the art of
marriage®
getting to the heart of God's design

FAMILYLIFE® presents

the art of marriage®

getting to the heart of God's design

FAMILYLIFE®
Little Rock, Arkansas

THE ART OF MARRIAGE®
FamilyLife Publishing®
5800 Ranch Drive
Little Rock, Arkansas 72223
1-800-FL-TODAY • FamilyLife.com
FLTI, d/b/a FamilyLife®, is a ministry of Campus Crusade for Christ International®

ISBN: 978-1-60200-411-5

Design: Brand Navigation, LLC
Photography: iStockphoto and BigStock

Printed in the United States of America

First Edition

17 16 15 14 13   5 6 7 8 9

FAMILYLIFE®
Help for today. Hope for tomorrow.

contents

INTRODUCTION 1

session one LOVE *Happens* 2

session two LOVE *Fades* 24

PROJECT 1 44

session three LOVE *Dances* 48

PROJECT 2 74

session four LOVE *Interrupted* 78

PROJECT 3 96

session five LOVE *Sizzles* 98

session six LOVE *Always* 122

NOTES 144

the art of ♥ marriage

This event was designed differently from most video marriage conferences, and much effort has been made to pattern this manual differently as well. What you are holding is not intended to simply give you the right answers; it's more about giving you a place to process life and capture your thoughts while you learn more about marriage at this event.

It is also a place to find more resources for later use. Many people go to an event, return home, and though they have good intentions of reviewing everything they learned, the book lands on a shelf, never to be opened again. Who hasn't been there? But we hope there is enough in this manual that you might even want to leave it out on the coffee table and occasionally thumb through it.

Inside, you'll find highlights of key concepts from the video, related articles, short exercises to take the teaching a bit deeper (and personalize it for *your* marriage), and even date-night suggestions, so you can follow up on each session in the weeks to come.

Marriage is truly an art. Whether you're just about to begin, or have been working on your canvas for years, we at FamilyLife believe that with continued effort and God's grace, your relationship is bound to become a masterpiece.

session **one**

LOVE Happens

God's Purpose and Plan

"The first bond of society is marriage."

—Cicero

the BIG brush strokes

- God designed marriage and has a great plan in mind.
- The primary purpose of marriage is to reflect God's glory.
- It is important to *receive your spouse* as God's perfect gift for you.

a kid's perspective[1]

Gwen, age nine: "When I get married I want to marry someone who is tall and handsome and rich and hates spinach as much as me."

Arnold, age six: "I want to get married, but not right away yet because I can't cross the street by myself yet."

Steven, age ten: "I want to marry somebody just like my mother except I hope she don't make me clean up my room."

Bobby, age nine: "First she has to like pizza, then she has to like cheesecake, after that she has to like fudge candy, then I know our marriage will last forever."

top reasons people marry

Love 91%[2]

Companionship 88%

To signify a lifelong commitment 82%

Security for children 79%

To make a public commitment to each other 77%

Legal status or for financial security 66%

Because of religious beliefs 62%

Response to family pressure 50%

Desire for a special occasion 45%

Many people choose marriage for good reasons, yet the divorce rates are still high. Why? Some idealize marriage; others underestimate the amount of effort it really takes to make a relationship work. With so many marriages failing, an increasing number of people are wondering if marriage is even worth the trouble. According to a 2002 survey on marriage and cohabitation,

- Approximately 28 percent of men and women cohabitated before their first marriage.[3]

- Among men and women who considered religion very important, more than 4 in 10 had cohabited at some time in their lives.[4]

"My concept of marriage was totally distorted because of what I knew of the music industry. People get married and divorced all the time.... When we got married, we talked about it, and because I had been married once before and divorced, I wasn't sure that I could be the husband I wanted to be.... I didn't trust myself. [When] I mentioned that to Julie, I said, 'Well, you know, we'll give it our best, and if it doesn't work, we'll go our separate ways.' And she [said,] 'No! This is it; there is no other one for me. This is the one, and this is the only one.' And I [thought,] 'Wow, what a concept.' It was completely new to me that there wasn't any way out."

—**Paul Overstreet,** songwriter and musician

If marriage so often ends in disillusionment and failure, why do people get married to begin with?

"[Because] we need a witness to our lives. There's a billion people on the planet.... What does any one life really mean? But in a marriage, you're promising to care about everything. The good things, the bad things, the terrible things, the mundane things... all of it, all the time, every day. You're saying 'Your life will not go unnoticed because I will notice it. Your life will not go un-witnessed because I will be your witness.'"

—**Beverly Clark,** from the movie *Shall We Dance?*

"She's got gaps, I got gaps, together we fill gaps."

—**Rocky Balboa,** from the movie *Rocky*

take it to heart

why DID you get married?

What are some of the reasons you married your spouse? Check all that apply; then rank the top three in order of priority.

- ☑ We were in love.
- ☐ I did not want to end up alone.
- ☐ My family thought I should.
- ☐ To experience a deeper spiritual intimacy.
- ☐ It seemed like the thing to do when you grow up.
- ☐ To have a good friend around.
- ☐ For sex.
- ☐ I wanted someone in my life to help make me a better person.
- ☐ For financial security.
- ☐ Because I wanted children.
- ☐ Because we already had children together.
- ☐ I thought my spouse would be a great parent.
- ☐ It sounded fun and exciting.
- ☐ I wanted a change in my life.
- ☐ Other: ______________________________

____

____

The purpose of marriage

- Marriage is not primarily about you.
- It is just as important to **BECOME** the right person as it is to **FIND** the right person.
- The myth of "The One" is not biblical. The one you married is the one with whom you are to make a life.

The ultimate purpose of marriage is to reflect God's image.

- Marriage reflects to the world God's promise to be with us and to redeem us.
- Marriage is a covenant—a permanent promise—not a contract.
- Marriage is more than a device to suit our own needs; it exists for a bigger purpose.

"'Therefore a man shall leave his father and mother and hold fast to his wife, and the two shall become one flesh.' This mystery is profound, and I am saying that it refers to Christ and the church."

—Ephesians 5:31–32

"Marriage is embedded in the culture as a gospel testimony that is always making statements. The only question is whether it's a good statement or a bad one."

—Dave Harvey

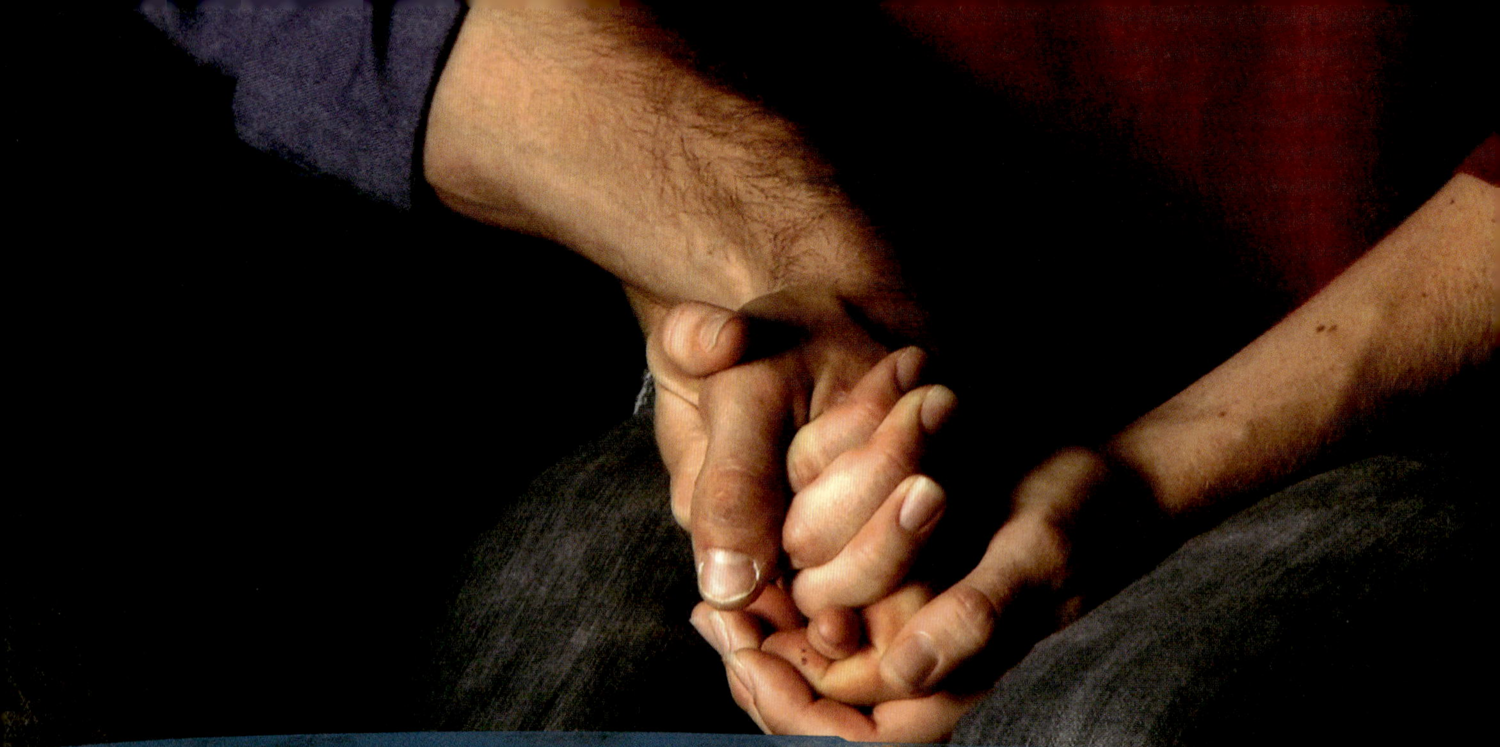

five things i wish i'd known before marriage[5]

by Dave Boehi

1) Marriage is not all about you. It's not about your happiness and self-fulfillment. It's not about getting your needs met. It's about going through life together and serving God together and serving each other.

2) You are about to learn a painful lesson—you are both very selfish people. This may be difficult to comprehend during the happy and hazy days of courtship, but it's true, and it shocks many couples during their first years of marriage.

3) The person you love the most is also the person who can hurt you the deepest. That's the risk and pain of marriage. And the beauty of marriage is working through your hurt and pain and resolving your conflicts and solving your problems.

4) You can't make it work on your own. It's obvious that marriage is difficult—just look at how many couples today end [up] in divorce. To make your marriage last for a lifetime, you need to rely on God for the power and love and strength and wisdom and endurance you need.

5) Never stop enjoying each other. Always remember that marriage is an incredible gift to be enjoyed. Ecclesiastes 9:9 says, "Enjoy life with the woman whom you love all the days of your fleeting life which He has given to you under the sun; for this is your reward in life and in your toil in which you have labored under the sun" (NASB).

God created marriage and designed it with a specific purpose and plan. But ignoring His design leads to chaos, confusion, pain, and suffering. Music also has a "design" by which a composer creates a piece.

However, John Cage, a twentieth-century composer, believed the world was the result of random chance, with no Creator behind its design. As a result, he applied the same theory to the creation of his music, flipping coins to determine which notes should be played. The music was very difficult to follow and often incited boos from the crowd (and sometimes even the musicians!). Why didn't this work? The human heart longs for order and beauty, yet chaos leaves the heart restless and unresolved.

Oddly enough, Cage did not apply his own theory of chance to his favorite hobby of mushroom gathering. Even he was wise enough to recognize that if he randomly picked mushrooms for eating, there would soon be no John Cage![6]

God's plan for marriage

[18] Then the LORD God said, "It is not good that the man should be alone; I will make him a helper fit for him." [19] Now out of the ground the LORD God formed every beast of the field and every bird of the heavens and brought them to the man to see what he would call them. And whatever the man called every living creature, that was its name. [20] The man gave names to all livestock and to the birds of the heavens and to every beast of the field. But for Adam there was not found a helper fit for him. [21] So the LORD God caused a deep sleep to fall upon the man, and while he slept took one of his ribs and closed up its place with flesh. [22] And the rib that the LORD God had taken from the man he made into a woman and brought her to the man. [23] Then the man said, "This at last is bone of my bones and flesh of my flesh; she shall be called Woman, because she was taken out of Man." [24] Therefore a man shall leave his father and his mother and hold fast [cleave] to his wife, and they shall become one flesh.

—Genesis 2:18–24

a unique gift

- Eve's creation was different from the animals' creation; clearly, she was special!
- *Ishah* is the Hebrew word for "woman," and *ish* is the Hebrew word for "man." Adam made a distinction in his naming of Eve.
- Just as Eve was a gift to Adam, your spouse is a **gift** from God.

receiving your spouse

- "Receiving your spouse" means more than "accepting" him or her; it means you embrace the God-given differences He's built into each of you.
- It's remembering every day that moment you joined together at the altar—each a special gift to the other.
- Your spouse is not your enemy.
- Receiving your spouse is a DAILY choice.

schulte's tips on receiving

- Look for the very tip of the ball, which requires **focus** and **concentration**.
- "Look the ball" **all the way** into your hands, until you have it **firmly grasped**.
- Quickly tuck it into the crook of your arm. Keep looking at it until it is **fully tucked**.
- Finally, **look up** and get set to run! (If you're not already smashed into the ground.)

What if I was previously married?

The important thing is *not* to be concerned with the state of any previous marriages, but rather to focus on the strength of your commitment to the marriage you are in *today*. You cannot change what happened in the past, but you can begin transforming your present marriage into one that honors Christ.

staying connected in the valley

by Pam Mutz

The loss of a child, and other tragedies, can be very difficult to work through with your spouse. However, many couples find that the process of working through a tragedy draws them closer together. The following are a few ways you can stay connected to your spouse in the midst of heartache:

1) Spend time reading the Word of God both individually and as a couple, particularly the book of Psalms.

2) Pray together. Use scriptures to enrich your prayer time. Husbands, choose to initiate.

3) Journaling is a concrete way to express to God how you feel and helps a spouse understand your struggle.

4) Worship corporately with other believers, even when you don't feel like it.

5) Join a small group so that others can support and encourage you as you walk through this difficult time.

6) Practice a family tradition that commemorates your loved one, such as releasing balloons into the air or writing a love letter to that person.

7) Choose to find joy in other areas of life, and verbalize a thankful heart. Make a written list of the things you're thankful for. True joy in a family is caught, not taught.

8) Go away together as a couple and regroup. Some things can't be sorted out in the midst of children, jobs, and routine. Take a weekend to process, cry, hold each other, communicate, and rest.

9) Embrace the Holy Spirit as your Comforter, and allow him to work as you rest.

10) Verbalize your choice to make your attitude better, not bitter.

11) Ask for help from trusted friends or a counselor.

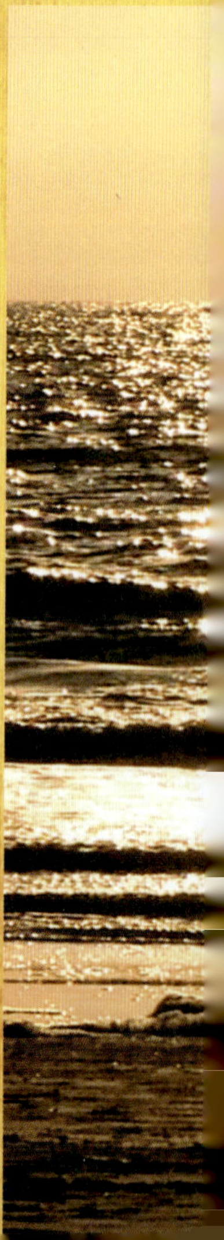

THEREFORE shall a MAN leave his father and his mother, and shall CLEAVE unto his WIFE: and THEY shall be ONE flesh.

GENESIS 2:24 (KJV)

on your own

receiving your spouse

What are the top three difficulties or problems you've experienced since you've been married?

1)

2)

3)

How have these trials affected your ability to continue receiving your spouse? To view him or her as God's special gift to you?

did i choose the right person?

Some couples, after facing greater problems and differences in personalities than they anticipated, begin to wonder, "Did I choose the right person?" They might think, *Things would be easier if I had just married a person who better understands me.*

But the question is not "Did I *marry* the right person?" Rather, one must ask, "Am I *becoming* the right person?"

> **"I have no way of knowing whether or not [you] married the wrong [person], but I do know that many people have a lot of wrong ideas about marriage and what it takes to make that marriage happy and successful. I'll be the first to admit that it's possible that you did marry the wrong person. However, if you treat the wrong person like the right person, you could well end up having married the right person after all. On the other hand, if you marry the right person, and treat that person wrong, you certainly will have ended up marrying the wrong person. I also know that it is far more important to *be* the right *kind* of person than it is to marry the right person. In short, whether you married the right or wrong person is primarily up to *you*."**
>
> **—Zig Ziglar,** *Courtship After Marriage*

leaving, cleaving, and becoming one

- **Leaving** means to shift loyalties from your parents to a new set of loyalties with your spouse.
- A commitment to being married is a commitment to no longer being emotionally and physically dependent on one's parents.
- **Cleaving** is a permanent relational bond, like two metals melted together, forming a new alloy . . . "becoming one."
- Cleaving must be a continual act you engage in throughout your married life. It does not happen automatically just because you said words at an altar on your wedding day.

"The failure to shift loyalty from parents to spouse is a central issue in almost all marital conflict."

—Dan Allender and Tremper Longman III, *Intimate Allies*

more insight

Leave: In this first marriage ceremony, the word translated as "leave" also has the idea of "abandoning" or "leaving behind." A new husband is called to establish a new home and a new family allegiance, with his wife as his companion.

Cleave: The union of two people in marriage is so strong, the word *cleave* (meaning "to cling" or "stick to") is used to describe what happens. Job used the same word when he said, "My bones stick to my skin and to my flesh" (Job 19:20). This implies that the union is inseparable, as Jesus said in Matthew 19:6: "What therefore God has joined together, let no man separate" (NASB).

Become one flesh: Just as Adam and Eve were united in their flesh (because Eve was fashioned from Adam's rib), a couple is now of the same body, an idea the apostle Paul highlighted in Ephesians 5:28, encouraging husbands to "love their own wives as their own bodies" (NASB).

the cost of a wedding

- The average amount a couple in the United States actually spends on a wedding, *excluding* the honeymoon and the engagement ring, is $19,581. This is 50 percent higher than the typical budget a couple sets for their wedding.[7]
- Premarital-counseling costs range from $100 to $750, depending on the extent of the counseling—a paltry sum compared to the cost of the wedding.[8]
- Couples who undergo premarital counseling have a 31 percent lower divorce rate than those who do not.[9]

Vows are important because they reflect the very character of God, who promises to never "leave you or forsake you" (Deuteronomy 31:6). **His love is everlasting, unconditional, and never failing.**

A TRADITIONAL WEDDING VOW	WHAT IT MEANS ON THE WEDDING DAY	WHAT IT REALLY MEANS
"With God as my witness . . ."	Lord help us . . .	This is a solemn vow before God and man.
"I take you . . ."	I can't believe someone would marry me!	I receive you, *unconditionally*, as God's perfect gift for me.
"To be my wife/husband"	Finally, someone who understands me.	I am no longer alone—I'm in this for good.
"To have and to hold"	Hopefully "to hold" includes more than just "holding . . ."	To be close physically, emotionally, and spiritually
"From this day forward"	Wow . . . this is seriously happening!	The wedding is a sprint at the start of a marathon.
"For better or for worse"	Things are only getting better . . . right?	There will be good times, there will be hard times, and there will be really hard times, and we will go through them together.
"In sickness and in health"	Who gets sick these days? Only old people, right?	I will clean up after you when you are too sick to do it.
"To love and to cherish"	Love is such an amazing feeling; no one could ever stop feeling this way.	I will think of your needs as much as I think of my own (Philippians 2:3–4).
"'Til death do us part"	Die? We'll never die!	Death comes much too soon.

God designed marriage to be a covenant, not a contract. What's the difference?

CONTRACT	COVENANT
Based on legalism and leverage	Based on love and loyalty
Lasts "as long as we both shall love"	Lasts "as long as we both shall live"
Calls for the signing of names	Calls for the binding of hearts

"I didn't marry you because you were perfect. . . . I married you because you gave me a promise. That promise made up for your faults. And the promise I gave you made up for mine. Two imperfect people got married, and it was the promise that made the marriage. And when our children were growing up, it wasn't a house that protected them; and it wasn't our love that protected them; it was that promise."

—Thornton Wilder, *The Skin of Our Teeth*

take it to heart

receiving your spouse as God's gift

Your spouse is a gift to you from God. What are some of the qualities that first attracted you to your spouse, or that you appreciate now? *(Check all that apply.)*

- ❑ Pays attention to detail
- ❑ Remains calm in tense situations
- ❑ Likes to have fun
- ❑ Is well organized
- ❑ Stays focused on a task
- ❑ Loves to spend time getting to know people
- ❑ Is good at getting a project off the ground
- ❑ Wants to work through disagreements
- ❑ Expresses feelings well
- ❑ Likes to talk
- ❑ Looks good in jeans
- ❑ Looks good out of jeans
- ❑ Loves to be spontaneous
- ❑ Can really throw a party
- ❑ Gives generously
- ❑ Seemed like he/she would make a great parent
- ❑ Gives wise counsel
- ❑ Is easy to please
- ❑ Works hard
- ❑ Other: ______________________________

____

____

COMPLETING the Picture

- I must receive my spouse as God's perfect gift for me.
- I must choose to believe that my spouse is not my enemy.
- I must renew my commitment to the permanency of marriage.
- I affirm that the primary purpose of my marriage is to reflect the glory of God.

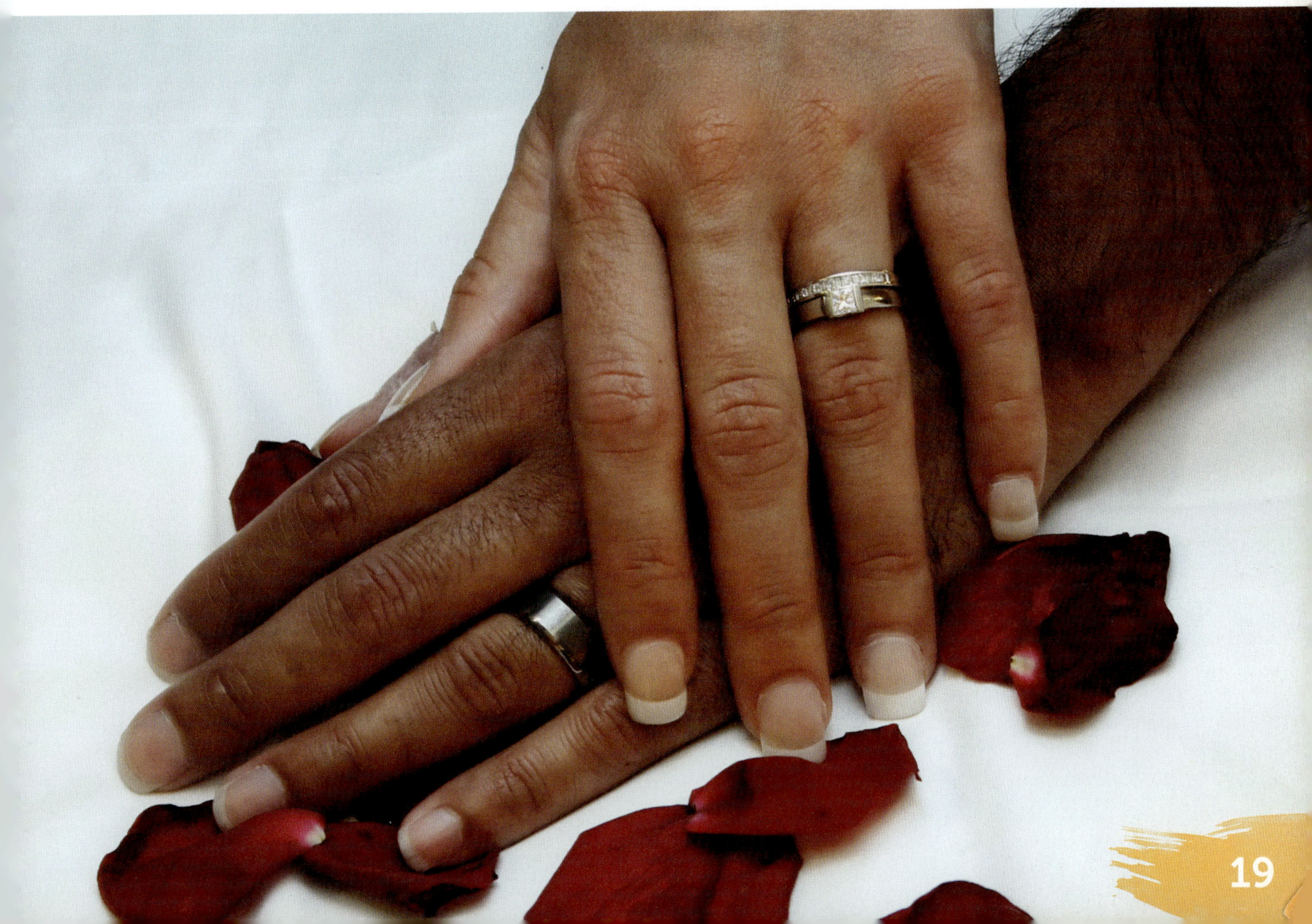

after the event

Date-Night Ideas

- Go to the restaurant that was your favorite when you were dating, or one similar to it.
- Re-create the evening of your proposal, or as close to it as you can get.
- Go through your wedding album and reread your wedding invitation and vows. Think about the words.
- Watch your wedding video.

Date-Night Discussion

1) What did you find helpful in this session on the subject of love and why people get married?
2) What is your favorite memory from your wedding day?
3) What about your marriage reflects God's glory? What doesn't?
4) Did you really leave your parents—emotionally, physically, and financially—and bond with each other? If not, what steps can you take to do so now?
5) Each of you take turns saying, "You are the only one for me. I am committed to you for life. You are God's gift to me."
6) Follow this by asking, "What can I do this week to help you feel and understand that more?"

Date-Night Prayer

God, help us to receive each other as a gift from You to be treasured and celebrated. Thank You for bringing us together. Help us to grow together more and more. Amen.

respectfully leaving your parents[10]

by Dennis and Barbara Rainey

You may have moved out, but have you really left your parents behind?

God did not mince words when instructing a married couple to leave their parents. The Hebrew words used in Genesis 2:24 (KJV), which states that "a man shall leave his father and his mother and shall cleave unto his wife," mean "to forsake dependence upon," "let loose," "leave behind," "release," and "let go."

Later, Jesus addressed the issue when He said that no one was ever intended to come between a husband and a wife (Matthew 19:6). No one! No in-laws, no mother, no father was meant to divide a couple who had made a covenant with each other to leave, cleave, and become one flesh.

This pointed instruction is needed. Psychologist Dan Allender says in the book *Intimate Allies* that "the failure to shift loyalty from parents to spouse is a central issue in almost all marital conflict."[11]

God knows that leaving parents will always be a difficult transition, especially in homes where the child-parent bond has been solid and warm. Unfortunately, many (if not most) couples do not cut the apron strings—they lengthen them!

What Leaving Looks Like

After our wedding ceremony, Barbara and I walked down the church aisle together, symbolically proclaiming to all those witnesses that we had left our parents. We had forsaken our dependence upon them for our livelihood and emotional support and were turning to each other as the primary relationship of our lives. The public affirmation of our covenant to each other meant, "No relationship on earth, other than my relationship with Jesus Christ and God, is more important than my relationship with my spouse."

If we do not leave our parents correctly, we will be like a couple I knew who were dependent financially on the wife's family. The situation was robbing the husband of his family leadership potential. The wife kept looking to her dad to bail them out after poor choices. Her husband wasn't able to grow up, face his responsibility to make correct choices for his family, and live with the consequences of his decisions. He was losing self-respect as a man, and it was undermining his wife's respect for him as well.

It can be equally destructive to continue to be emotionally dependent on a parent. This dependence will hinder the Super Glue–like bonding that must occur between husband and wife.

How to Leave, Yet Still Honor, Your Parents

Leaving your home does not mean you permanently withdraw and no longer have a good relationship with your parents. That's isolating yourself from your parents, not leaving. The commandment in Exodus 20:12 to honor your parents means that when you leave them, you need to go with respect, love, admiration, and affirmation for their sacrifices and efforts in raising you. But you must make a break from them and sever your dependence on them. As time passes, you must be diligent to prevent any reestablishment of dependence at critical points in your marriage.

Leaving certain kinds of parents requires special sensitivity. For example, if your mom or dad is a single parent, she or he may no longer have anyone at home to lean on and may feel terribly alone. Or perhaps you left behind a parent who endures a lifeless marriage devoid of passion. In either case, your leaving has created a big void in the home. Nevertheless, you must sever the ties.

You can honor your parents and also reap benefits by seeking their wisdom on certain issues. When you ask them to offer their insights, you must make it clear that you are seeking information and advice, not surrendering your right to make final decisions. A tip: Always try to consult your spouse before seeking input from parents. Give yourselves some time to become good at this. You may have depended on your parents for twenty years but have been married only one!

When Parents Want to Reattach

Sometimes without realizing it, we may allow our parents to reestablish the severed connections. It could occur during a Christmas visit. It might happen during a phone call when the child mentions to the parent some disappointment or failure experienced in the marriage relationship.

I remember how, early in our marriage, I shared a weakness about Barbara with my mother. Now my mom is a great mother, but I was astounded at how she rushed to my side, like a mother hen coming to aid her wounded little chick. Her response startled me. I told Barbara about it and apologized. I promised I would not again discuss negative things about her with my mom.

You must not allow parents to innocently (or not so innocently) drive a wedge between you and your spouse. Some parents may seek to manipulate and control their child. For example, a father won't stop telling his "little girl" what to do. The husband may need to step in and explain to his wife how destructive this is to the health of the marriage. Boundaries limiting the amount of communication between father and daughter may need to be installed for the long or short term.

Or a mother may be trying to call the shots with her son. The wife needs to explain carefully to her husband what she is observing. If the situation doesn't improve, there may need to be a cooling-off period when the husband minimizes contact with his mother and directs his attention toward his wife.

These showdowns may be intimidating for either spouse, but boundaries need clarification. You may need to call on an older mentor for advice before you take action, but your allegiance must first and foremost be to your spouse.

At this point, I want to encourage you husbands to be "the man" and protect your wife. Sometimes you may need to graciously but firmly step in and shield her from a manipulative parent, but I implore you to guard gently your wife's heart and your marriage from a dad or mom whose intentions may be good but counterproductive.

If as a couple you are having trouble maintaining a clean break, you may decide to spend less time at home for holiday visits. Instead of a week, perhaps the stay should be shortened to two or three days. Or skip a holiday altogether, just as a way of clarifying where your primary commitment lies.

A way to forestall some misunderstandings and help with decision making is to determine your family's values early in the marriage. For instance, one value may be establishing your own family's Christmas traditions as your children leave infancy. Having a clear idea of what you are doing and why will make it easier to explain your choices to parents.

As your parents grow older, they may need your assistance. Again, approach this issue prayerfully as a team. Take as much time as you can to make decisions, especially those with long-term ramifications. Some choices will be very difficult, but in most cases, the health of the marriage must take precedence. Although you must consider the financial situation, too, a parent may need to live at a retirement center instead of with you, if the parent's presence will adversely affect your marriage.

One final thing to keep in mind: Leaving is not a one-time event or limited to the early years of marriage. The temptation to reconnect some of the old bonding lines will continue as long as parents are alive. For example, when grandchildren come along, most parents want to share from their vast stores of experience on how to raise kids.

Both parents and their children need to remain on guard so that leaving remains just that—a healthy, God-ordained realignment of the parent-child relationship.

session **two**

LOVE Fades

Overcoming Isolation

"We must never be naïve enough to think of marriage as a safe harbor from the Fall. . . . The deepest struggles of life will occur in the most primary relationship affected by the Fall: marriage."

—Dan Allender and Tremper Longman III, *Intimate Allies*

the BIG brush strokes

- Couples naturally drift toward isolation.
- Our differences and weaknesses can push us apart.
- Sin has affected every marriage.
- The gospel brings healing and reconciliation.
- Couples must learn to walk by the power of the Holy Spirit in marriage.

He Said . . .

"I thought I was doing great as a husband. . . . I would have said to you [that] on a scale of 1 to 10, my marriage is probably a 10. If not a 10, it's a 9.8, and I guarantee you my wife would agree." —Dave Wilson

She Said . . .

"And I would have said, 'We're a 1.0, maybe like a 0.5,' and I think he was totally clueless . . . which made me even more angry, because I'm thinking, *How do you not know how bad we're doing?*" —Ann Wilson

Art and marriage are both studies in contrasts: A good painting might combine the bitter shades of brown with the brightest hues of blue. Art draws together the harsh and the soft and holds both in tension. It recognizes the pain, yet it also celebrates the joys of life. Good art requires patience and skill; it is a beauty to behold, and masterpieces are often the fruit of a lifetime of labor. Most marriages begin with the hope of discovery and the joy of sharing life together, yet not every marriage becomes a masterpiece. What happens? What goes wrong?

the drift toward isolation

- One reason couples drift apart is that they fail to make their marriage the priority it ought to be.
- We are culturally conditioned to believe that our happiness ought to be our number-one priority in life.
- Selfishness is one of the root causes of isolation.

"Unless you lovingly and energetically nurture and maintain your marriage, you will begin to drift apart from your mate. You'll live together, but you will live alone."

—Dennis and Barbara Rainey, *Staying Close*

"The devil's strategy for our times is to trivialize human existence and to isolate us from one another while creating the delusion that the reasons are time pressures, work demands, or economic anxieties."

—Dr. Phillip Zombardo, "The Age of Indifference," *Psychology Today*

"The good news is that isolation can be defeated. Its disease can be cured if you are willing to make the right choices and then put the necessary effort into building oneness."

—Dennis and Barbara Rainey, *Staying Close*

Researcher John Gottman, after interviewing thousands of couples, said that there are four behaviors he calls "The Four Horsemen of the Apocalypse," whose presence in a marriage indicates a high probability of divorce. These behaviors are "criticism, contempt, defensiveness, and withdrawal." Once these behaviors take over, "unless a couple makes changes, they are likely to find themselves sliding helplessly toward the end of their marriage."[1]

take it to heart

what has caused you to drift apart?

1) At this point in your marriage, compared to when you first married, do you feel you've become more isolated or more connected? Explain.

On the following scale, circle the mark that indicates where you were when you first married, and draw a box around the mark that indicates where you are now.

connected —|—|—|—|—|—|—|—|—|—|—|—|—|—|— **isolated**

2) As you consider married couples who have stayed together, what have you seen them do to resist the natural drift toward isolation?

"Genesis 3 marks the transition from a sinless state of humanity, in union with God and in fellowship with Him and walking with His blessing and approval and pleasure, to a state where there is sin, and Adam and Eve are alienated from God."

—Wayne Grudem

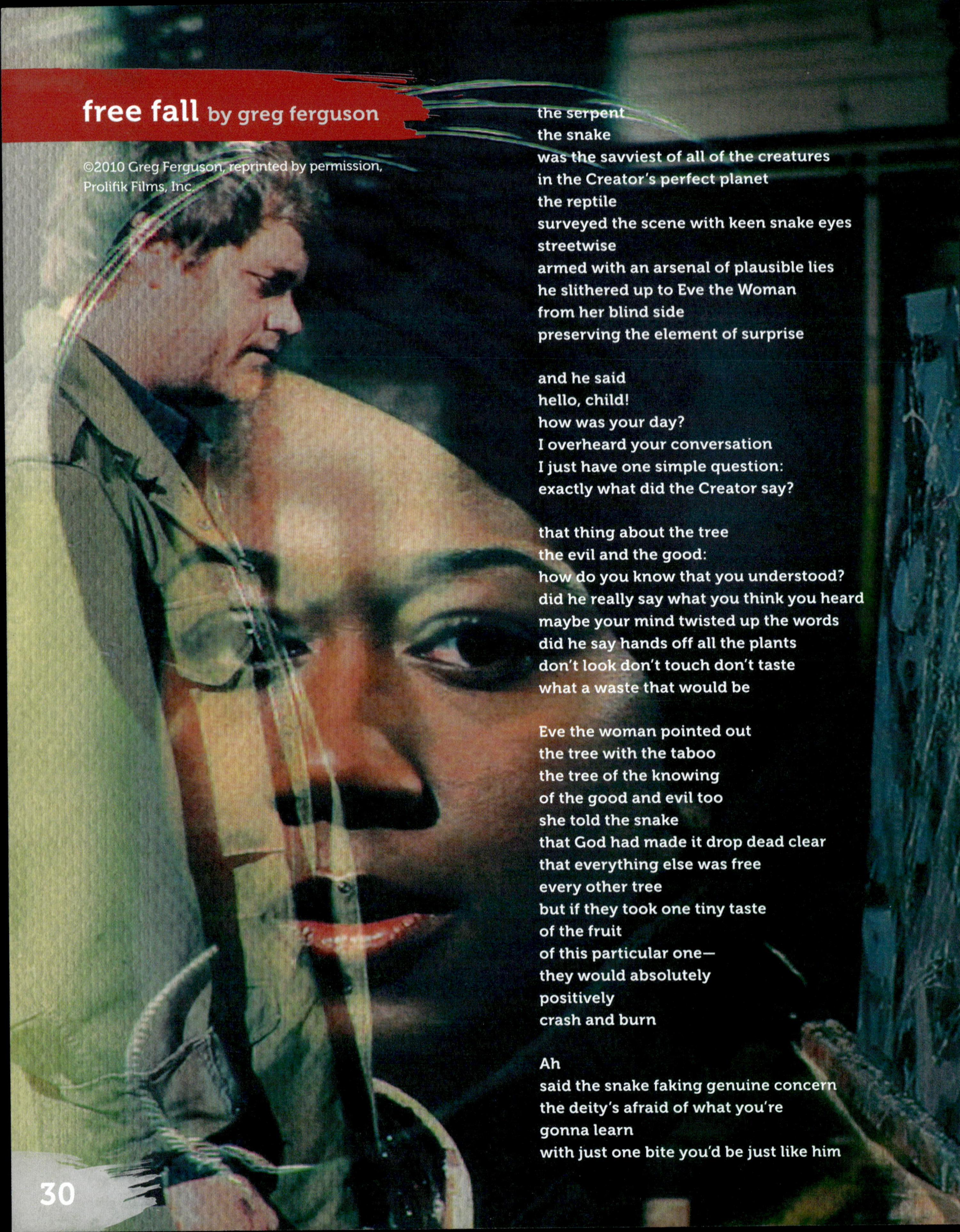

free fall by greg ferguson

the serpent
the snake
was the savviest of all of the creatures
in the Creator's perfect planet
the reptile
surveyed the scene with keen snake eyes
streetwise
armed with an arsenal of plausible lies
he slithered up to Eve the Woman
from her blind side
preserving the element of surprise

and he said
hello, child!
how was your day?
I overheard your conversation
I just have one simple question:
exactly what did the Creator say?

that thing about the tree
the evil and the good:
how do you know that you understood?
did he really say what you think you heard
maybe your mind twisted up the words
did he say hands off all the plants
don't look don't touch don't taste
what a waste that would be

Eve the woman pointed out
the tree with the taboo
the tree of the knowing
of the good and evil too
she told the snake
that God had made it drop dead clear
that everything else was free
every other tree
but if they took one tiny taste
of the fruit
of this particular one—
they would absolutely
positively
crash and burn

Ah
said the snake faking genuine concern
the deity's afraid of what you're
gonna learn
with just one bite you'd be just like him

eyes wide open
knowing the heights of what humans can do
knowing the depths, the despicable too
God would have no tactical advantage over you
you and your man
could have the run of the place
total control over the food you eat
the life you live
the path you choose;
with just one small bite
you could gain the whole green world
and that means that God of yours
would lose

the woman Eve walked closer
and closer to the tree
she sniffed and felt the fruit
against her cheek

"totally wise with open eyes"—she said—
what's wrong with that?
"maybe my man and I
were born for this
born to know
born to control
born to rule"

she swallowed hard
and it was done
she gave some
to her covenant partner Adam
he opened his mouth
and gobbled it down
and the universe

was silent

it was the cool part of the day
and God was walking
walking
through the land he made
his ecosystem
so magnificently put together
about to erode
about to implode
before his sad and timeless eyes—
he took one long last look
and kissed the innocence
goodbye

Adam
where you hiding son
Eve
girl what have you done

look around
it's broken now
under a curse
from bad to worse

now your eyes are wise and clear
now you know shame
now you know fear
now you know you're naked
now you run for cover

here's what gonna happen:

life will be shorter
pain will be greater
work will be harder
grinding it out
by the sweat on your brow
the blood on your hands

Eve and Adam
even the bond you have
will now be strained
slightly off
distorted
reframed

and as for you
reptile
snake
Adam will crush your head
you will strike and bite his heel
you will feel the weight
of the consequences of what
you've done for eons

he looked them in the eye
with a sigh
it's broken now, he said

and the serpent

he just smiled

Genesis 3:1–16 (emphasis added)

1 Now the serpent was more crafty than any other beast of the field that the LORD God had made.

He said to the woman, "Did God actually say, 'You shall not eat of any tree in the garden'?"
2 And the woman said to the serpent, "We may eat of the fruit of the trees in the garden, 3 but
God said, 'You shall not eat of the fruit of the tree that is in the midst of the garden, neither
shall you touch it, lest you die.'" 4 But the serpent said to the woman, "You will not surely die.
5 For God knows that when you eat of it your eyes will be opened, and you will be like God,
knowing good and evil." 6 So when the woman saw that the tree was good for food, and that
it was a delight to the eyes, and that the tree was to be desired to make one wise, **she took of
its fruit and ate, and she also gave some to her husband who was with her, and he ate.**

THE RESULTS OF THEIR SIN WERE . . .

Shame

7 Then the eyes of both were opened, **and they knew that they were naked**. And they sewed fig leaves together and made themselves loincloths.

Guilt

8 And they heard the sound of the LORD God walking in the garden in the cool of the day, and **the man and his wife hid themselves from the presence of the LORD God** among the trees of the garden.

Fear

9 But the LORD God called to the man and said to him, "Where are you?" 10 And he said, "I heard
the sound of you in the garden, and **I was afraid, because I was naked, and I hid myself.**"

Blame Shifting

11 He said, "Who told you that you were naked? Have
you eaten of the tree of which I commanded you
not to eat?" 12 The man said, "The woman whom you
gave to be with me, she gave me fruit of the tree,
and I ate." 13 Then the LORD God said to the woman,
"What is this that you have done?" The woman said,
"The serpent deceived me, and I ate."

14 The LORD God said to the serpent,
"Because you have done this,
cursed are you above all livestock
and above all beasts of the field;
on your belly you shall go,
and dust you shall eat
all the days of your life."

Battle for Control

15 "I will put enmity between you and the woman,
and between your offspring and her offspring;
he shall bruise your head,
and you shall bruise his heel."
16 To the woman he said,
"I will surely multiply your pain in childbearing;
in pain you shall bring forth children.
Your desire shall be for your husband,
and he shall rule over you."

the fallout from the fall

- Pride and disobedience were behind Adam and Eve's rejection of God's plan in the garden (Genesis 3:1–6).
- By rejecting God's plan, Adam and Eve's relationship, intimacy, and unity with God were broken.
- Sin now infects and affects everyone.
- **A result of sin:** blame shifting. Adam blamed Eve for his own sin. Eve blamed the serpent for her sin. Adam also blamed God ("the woman whom *you* gave to me . . ."[3:12]).
- The result of sin was punishment in three parts:
  - Pain in work (3:17–19)
  - Pain in childbirth (3:16)
  - Pain in marriage relationships (3:16)
- Another result of sin was marital conflict.
- Instead of *completing* each other, Adam and Eve began to *compete* with each other.
- There is a spiritual battle occurring within marriage:

"For we do not wrestle against flesh and blood, but against the rulers, against the authorities, against the cosmic powers over this present darkness, against the spiritual forces of evil in the heavenly places." —Ephesians 6:12

"Finally, be strong in the Lord and in the strength of his might. ***Put on the whole armor of God,*** *that you may be able to stand against the schemes of the devil."* —Ephesians 6:10–11

there is an enemy, and it is not your spouse.

"Differences are God's way of sanding off our rough edges."

—Bryan Carter

on your own

a futile feud?

Sometimes big arguments have small beginnings. The famous Hatfield-McCoy feud between two families on the West Virginia-Kentucky border lasted thirteen years and resulted in more than a dozen deaths. The reason for the bad blood? Many believe the most heated part of the battle began over the ownership of a pig.

When was the last time you had a big argument with your spouse that started over something small? What do you think was the deeper issue behind that argument?

It's the little things . . .

1) List some of the ways you are different from your spouse in two or three of the following areas:

- Family background
- Personality
- Education
- Interests
- Ways you use your free time
- Entertainment choices
- Spending habits

2) The Bible says that "two are better than one" (Ecclesiastes 4:9). In the space below, write down one way in which your spouse's differences have ultimately been a benefit to you.

"To be able to look forward to a lifelong, thriving marriage, you must have a clear understanding of the gospel. Without it, you cannot see God, yourself, or your marriage for what they truly are. The gospel is the fountain of a thriving marriage."

—**Dave Harvey,**
When Sinners Say "I Do"

the problem . . . and the solution

"G. K. Chesterton once responded to a newspaper article inviting readers all over the globe to answer the age-old question, 'What's wrong with the world?' His reply was brief and to the point, 'I am.'"

—quoted in Dave Harvey, *When Sinners Say "I Do"*

"Sin is wrong, not because of what it does to me, or my spouse, or child, or neighbor, but because it is an act of rebellion against the infinitely holy and majestic God."

—Jerry Bridges, *The Discipline of Grace*

The underlying aspect of all conflict in life and marriage is that we have rejected God's authority and leadership in our lives.

"All we like sheep have gone astray; we have turned—every one—to his own way." —Isaiah 53:6

"For all have sinned and fall short of the glory of God." —Romans 3:23

"The problem that we have is a sin problem. We have habit patterns that need to be addressed that contribute to our problems, but the root issue is sin, and that must be dealt with."

—Crawford Loritts

Christ came to free us from our addiction to self and our slavery to sin.

"For I delivered to you as of first importance what I also received: that Christ died for our sins in accordance with the Scriptures, that he was buried, that he was raised on the third day

in accordance with the Scriptures, and that he appeared to Cephas, then to the twelve. Then he appeared to more than five hundred brothers at one time." —1 Corinthians 15:3–6

"In Christ God was reconciling the world to himself, not counting their trespasses against them, and entrusting to us the message of reconciliation." —2 Corinthians 5:19

Jesus died and was raised to life again to purchase new life for us.

"God shows his love for us in that while we were still sinners, Christ died for us." —Romans 5:8

"What the cross brings is fresh starts and new beginnings." —Paul David Tripp

"Therefore, if anyone is in Christ, he is a new creation. The old has passed away; behold, the new has come." —2 Corinthians 5:17

We can have a relationship with Jesus Christ by trusting what He has done for us.

"For by grace you have been saved through faith. And this is not your own doing; it is the gift of God, not a result of works, so that no one may boast." —Ephesians 2:8–9

We trust in Christ by exercising faith (Hebrews 11:6).

- By faith we agree with God that we have turned away from His plan—we have sinned (Romans 3:23).
- By faith we turn from our sin and embrace God's forgiveness (Acts 26:18).
- By faith we embrace God's plan for our lives (John 10:10).

"The gospel of Christ crucified for our sins is the foundation of our lives. Marriage exists to display it. And when marriage breaks down, the gospel is there to forgive and heal and sustain until he comes, or until he calls."

—John Piper,
This Momentary Marriage

take it to heart

what every marriage needs

1) How important has God been in your life and marriage?

1	2	3	4	5	6	7	8	9	10

NOT IMPORTANT AT ALL — **VERY IMPORTANT**

2) Do you desire for God to play a greater role in your life and marriage?

3) If so, what needs to change in your life for this to happen?

4) Examine the fruit of the Spirit in Galatians 5:22–23:

Love, joy, peace, patience, kindness, goodness, faithfulness, gentleness, and self-control

Which of these attributes need to grow in your life? Circle your top two.

Identifying areas of growth in your life is important, but ultimately, it is the Holy Spirit who brings true spiritual fruit to bear in the life of a follower of Jesus.

COMPLETING the Picture

- I must learn how to resist the natural drift toward isolation in marriage.
- My individual sin is the issue behind marital conflict. I must learn to take responsibility for my sin and reconcile with God.
- Jesus Christ's sacrifice reconciled me to God and allows me to live in peace with Him and others.
- I must learn to walk each day by the power of the Holy Spirit in order to stay close to my spouse.

after the event

Date-Night Ideas

- As a couple, take a picnic to a place that says "isolation" to you (a field, an empty parking lot, an empty beach).
- Spend two hours on the couch together one evening, without the TV, cell phones, or the Internet. Just spend time together, talking and reading or just sitting quietly together. *For extra credit:* Do this again the following week, but spend the first twenty minutes in silence. Afterward, discuss how that separation made you feel.
- Face each other in the center of an empty football field. Slowly take a step apart from each other, keeping the same pace. Periodically say, "I love you," never raising your voice, and pay attention to when you can no longer hear the words.

Date-Night Discussion

1) What did you find helpful in the video, and in this manual, on the subject of love fading?

2) Do you routinely sin in a way that harms your marriage? (Each of you answer. Be open to your spouse's answer.)

3) What part do you believe God plays in keeping your marriage together? How could you and your spouse incorporate Him more into your lives and your marriage?

4) What is one thing you can do this week to help your spouse feel closer to you? (Each of you answer.)

Date-Night Prayer

Father, we are sinful. Forgive us. We long to be closer, but our sin divides us again and again. Help us bridge that divide, Lord. Help us look forward to the future. Give us the strength to believe we can be all You've created us to be, and that our marriage will feel like a gift, every day. Amen.

building a spiritual foundation for your marriage[2]

by Dennis and Barbara Rainey

Marriage first and foremost is a spiritual relationship. It works best when two people are connected individually to their God, walking with Him, obeying him through Scripture, and praying as individuals and as a couple. If you push the spiritual dimension to the side, you are ignoring the very God who created marriage and the One who can help you make it work.

Three key ingredients of a dynamic Christian life have significance when applied to the oneness you are trying to achieve as a married couple. I'll state these in the form of questions:

1) Is Your Family Part of God's Family?

Today many people think they are in God's family because they go to church, generally live a good life, or consider themselves religious. Other people are not sure where they would spend eternity if they died today.

God's ideal plan is that both partners in a marriage know Him personally, that they are first part of His family before they try to build a family of their own.

2) Are Both of You Giving Christ Control?

Jesus Christ is already Lord of the universe, but He waits patiently to have you make Him Lord of your life through personal commitment. That means trusting Him in a way you may have never trusted Him before.

During our first Christmas as newlyweds, we were prompted by the Holy Spirit to do something different. Before we exchanged the few gifts that lay under our sparsely decorated tree, we sat down separately and wrote "Title Deeds to Our Lives." Coming honestly before God, each of us listed our treasured dreams, plans, and possessions that we wanted to "sign over" to God. Then we folded our sheets and sealed them in an envelope addressed "To God Our Father." We put the letters in our safety deposit box with other important items.

Eighteen years later we retrieved that envelope and reviewed what we had deeded to the Lord. Among other things, Barbara had listed "to be settled and stable; children—at least one boy and one girl—and Dennis." Dennis had mentioned "security; a healthy, big family—several boys—and Barbara." We realized how over the years God had continuously weaned us from perishable, unimportant things and increasingly attached us to what really counts: people and His Word. We also noted, with thanksgiving, how much more God had given us than we had given up for Him.

Where do you stand in giving God total control over your life?

3) Are Both of You Allowing the Holy Spirit to Guide and Empower Your Lives?

God sent the Holy Spirit to do even greater works on earth through us than those done by Christ. He was sent to glorify Christ as well as to be our Counselor, Advisor, Advocate, Defender, Director, and Guide. In short, if you are interested in living life as Jesus promised, and if you want a marriage where the two of you grow spiritually, then yielding to the Holy Spirit is vital.

Perhaps that's why being "filled with the Spirit" is not a suggestion; it is a clear command given by Paul in his letter to the Ephesians: "Do not get drunk with wine, for that is dissipation, but be filled with the Spirit" (5:18, NASB).

The results of being filled with the Spirit are holiness and joy. Paul described it as "speaking to one another in psalms and hymns and spiritual songs, singing and making melody with your heart to the Lord; always giving thanks for all things in the name of our Lord Jesus Christ to God, even the Father" (5:19–20, NASB).

The Holy Spirit Works

Each of us needs something in marriage to defeat our selfishness. On more than one occasion, I (Dennis) can recall wanting to be angry at Barbara and yet at the same time knowing that my body is a temple of God, and that the Holy Spirit lives in me with the same power that raised Christ from the dead. The Spirit helps me control my temper, my impatience, and my desire to say things I would later regret.

I still fail, but I have found that as I inwardly yield my will to God, the fruit of the Spirit (love, joy, peace, patience, etc.) grows within me, and these qualities move me inevitably toward a beautiful oneness with Barbara.

Why not stop and pray right now for God to fill you with the Holy Spirit? Turn to page 46 for guidance on how to pray for the Holy Spirit to fill you and guide your life. Your marriage will reflect the love of God as you allow Him to fill, control, and empower you.

project one

Receiving Your Spouse

In Genesis 2:23, Adam received Eve as God's perfect gift. Think again about the concept of receiving your spouse as you answer the following questions:

1) How has the concept of unconditionally receiving your spouse helped you think differently about your marriage?

2) If your spouse were to know that you see him or her as God's gift for a lifetime, how would that change the way you relate to your spouse?

3) For *remarried* couples: As you look back on your previous marriage, did you see your spouse as God's gift for a lifetime? How is your concept of receiving your spouse different now?

4) Write down at least three things about your spouse for which you are thankful.

resisting the drift

The Natural Drift Toward Isolation

5) What are three areas that have caused drift in your marriage?

6) Of these three areas, which one do you need to devote more attention to in order to keep from drifting further apart?

7) What one step can you take this week to grow closer in this area?

8) For *remarried* couples: What factors led to isolation in your previous marriage? What can you do in this marriage to avoid repeating the same patterns?

Every Marriage Needs Christ

A personal relationship with Jesus Christ is foundational in accepting one's spouse unconditionally, as God's perfect gift, and resisting the natural drift toward isolation.

Have you ever entered into a personal relationship with Jesus Christ? If not, take the time right now to commit to following Him as your Lord and Savior. You may want to silently pray the following words. (Note that this prayer is not a formula for becoming a Christian. We've included it to help you express the desires of your heart. Though words are important, God knows the condition and intentions of your heart.)

> *Lord Jesus, I need You. Thank You for dying on the cross for my sins. I acknowledge that I am a sinner separated from You. Please forgive me. I receive You as my Savior and Lord. Thank You for forgiving my sins and giving me eternal life. Please take control of my life. Make me the kind of person You want me to be. Amen.*

9) In which area of your marriage do you most need to be reminded of Jesus' example today? *(Circle one.)*

Forgiving
Being reconciled
Serving
Loving unconditionally
Sacrificing
Returning evil with good
Responding kindly to unloving words or actions
Praying for others who mistreat me
Giving generously to those in need
Showing compassion
Demonstrating humility
Other: ____________________

Jesus said that we will know a tree by its fruit (Luke 6:44). Galatians 5:19–23 compares the "works of the flesh" and the "fruit of the Spirit."

10) Looking at the different kinds of fruit listed on page 38, which would you say most accurately represents your life?

11) Which would your spouse say best represents your life?

12) Do you desire to change and ask God to give you His power to bear the fruit of the Spirit? ❑ YES ❑ NO ❑ MAYBE

If you answered yes to the previous question, take time now to ask the Holy Spirit to guide, fill, and direct you:

Dear Father, I confess that I have sought to control my own life, and as a result, I have sinned against You. Thank You for forgiving me in Christ. I want You to have complete control of my life. You have commanded me to be filled with the Holy Spirit (Ephesians 5:18) and have promised to fill me if I ask in faith. Please fill me with Your Spirit and make me the person You want me to be. Amen.

Galatians 5:16 says, "Walk by the Spirit, and you will not carry out the desire of the flesh" (NASB). The "desire of the flesh" reflects our ongoing addiction to our own interests, rather than seeking to please God or serve our spouse.

13) In what areas of your marriage do you need a renewed ability to walk by the Spirit? *(Check all that apply.)*

- ❑ The way we communicate with each other
- ❑ Our sexual intimacy
- ❑ How we relate to our parents and/or extended family
- ❑ The way we spend our free time
- ❑ Finding ways to connect spiritually
- ❑ Understanding how to raise our children
- ❑ How we handle our finances
- ❑ Intentionally honoring my spouse in front of others

14) Are you doing any of the following? *(Check all that apply.)*

- ❑ Praying together daily (apart from meals)
- ❑ Studying the Bible on my own
- ❑ Studying the Bible together
- ❑ Taking opportunities to tell others about Jesus
- ❑ Teaching our children about following Jesus
- ❑ Attending church regularly
- ❑ Praying for each other
- ❑ Having regular date nights

15) Which of the activities above would be the most beneficial for you and your spouse to begin in your marriage? Take a moment to consider when would be the best time to start doing one of these activities together.

16) In your remaining time together, discuss with your spouse questions 6 and 13, as well as any spiritually significant decisions you made during the session.

One final note: If you made a decision to either receive Jesus as your Lord and Savior or to ask the Holy Spirit to guide and fill you, then we encourage you to follow up with your pastor or the host of this event. Ask him or her to recommend additional resources to help you continue growing in your relationship with Jesus.

session **three**

LOVE Dances

Fulfilling Our Responsibilities

"Wives, understand and support your husbands in ways that show your support for Christ. . . . Husbands, go all out in your love for your wives, exactly as Christ did for the church. . . . This is a huge mystery, and I don't pretend to understand it all."

—Excerpts from Ephesians 5, *The Message*

the BIG brush strokes

- God designed different responsibilities for men and women in marriage.
- Though their responsibilities are different, men and women are still equal in value.
- God calls men to sacrificially love and lead their wives.
- God calls women to respect and support their husbands.

the dance

Fred Astaire and Ginger Rogers, who made ten films together, are often recognized as the most famous dancing duo in American film history. However, Astaire was initially reluctant to dance with Rogers, preferring to avoid becoming part of a dance team.

According to Astaire, when they were first teamed together, "Ginger had never danced with a partner before. She faked it an awful lot . . . but Ginger had style and talent and improved as she went along. She got so that after a while everyone else who danced with me looked wrong."[1]

Part of what made their performance so attractive was that Ginger Rogers "so convincingly conveyed . . . that [dancing with Fred Astaire was] the most thrilling and satisfying experience imaginable."[2]

Rogers and Astaire were world-class dancers—masters of their art—yet there is much to learn from their craft that applies to marriage. For instance, good dancing requires that each person know his or her role and play it well, as the following tips illustrate.

tips from the dance pros[3]

On Leading

- The man leads by giving: the correct weight changes, clear signals to indicate change of direction, shape of body and arm and eye movement.
- The man must not rush the lady. Otherwise she will panic and rush herself and the subsequent choreography will be ruined.
- A good leader does not push or pull to disturb the balance of the lady. A little lead goes a long way.
- The lady is like the flower and the man the vase. The leader is there to support the lady.
- He must be technically capable enough to direct the lady in the desired direction and give her the chance to present her own steps with ease.
- Finally, he must [help] the lady enjoy dancing.

"Don't forget that Ginger Rogers did everything [Fred Astaire] did, . . . backwards and in high heels."

—Bob Thaves, *Frank and Ernest*

finding the perfect spouse

Many people are on the prowl for the perfect partner, but who defines perfection?

When *Cosmopolitan* magazine invited readers in the United Kingdom to describe the **perfect man**, all manner of responses came flooding in:[4]

> *"Like mine with very short hair or shaven. Nice body, muscular. . . . Cheeky smile, oh and very good in bed."*
>
> *"Taller than me. Short or shaved hair. Tattoos. Piercings."*
>
> *"Mine would be taller than me, and cute smile—twinkle in the eye. I like men with curly or wavy hair. I like men [who] are confident—not cocky (these are often mixed up). Like a man who knows what he wants."*
>
> *"Long brown hair, black rimmed glasses, black skinny jeans, cardigans, [C]onverse."*
>
> *"My perfect guy would be sweet, kind, have an incredibly weird sense of humour like me, loves rock music . . . and going to gigs, would love to sit and giggle at horror films with me, would be creative and would be able to carry interesting conversations with me and just someone that I could have a good time with, someone that I'd want to spend time with. I couldn't care less about looks or how good in bed they are (that'd just be a bonus). I just want a guy with a good personality."*
>
> *"My perfect man is tall, lean, dark hair, sexy eyes, romantic and very loving. Luckily, I'm describing my husband."*
>
> *"I can describe mine in two words. Doesn't exist."*

Meanwhile, the *Sunday Times* of London pondered the question, "**What Makes an Ideal Woman?**" A handful of different writers were invited to weigh in on the subject:[5]

> *"I'll settle for a woman who can eat. A woman who doesn't poke her food around the plate and hide things under her knife. . . . If I truly love her, then I guess we could always work the food thing through. As long as she isn't always 'tired.' Men are either awake or asleep, but women are always 'exhausted.'"* **—Giles Coren**

> *"The most attractive attribute in a woman, the most melting, the most utterly winning, is gratitude."* **—A. A. Gill**

> *"The perfect woman would show far greater tolerance of her perfect man's habits. She would allow, for example . . . the following: sugar in tea; a healthy skepticism of yoga and/or arnica; at least one curry a week; nonorganic deodorant (i.e., stuff that works); and free rein in Blockbuster at least twice a year (free rein to include films with explosions in them). . . . She'd intuitively understand and accept that she was the less accomplished driver. And map reader."* **—Matt Rudd**

> *"Questing for the perfect woman is folly. A check list gets a man nowhere. Like buying property, you'll never find all you desire."* **—Tom Stubbs**

> *"All my life I've thought I've known what I was after, but I have never ended up with it—and what I have ended up with is a 5ft 2in Canadian blonde, who turns out to be ideal."* **—Dom Joly**

> *"The moment I stop believing my wife is my ideal woman, I guess it's over. . . . The whole absurdly wonderful, almost impossibly romantic thing about all marriages is that what you are saying to each other is: 'You and me, we're perfect.' . . . Choosing a mate is not like buying a car or a house. Until she comes along, we have no idea what we really like: my imagination couldn't hold a candle to the real thing. The best part of falling in love with Claire was discovering all the things I didn't know I wanted or needed."* **—Alex James**

"A person [who] says 'I'll meet you halfway' is a poor judge of distance."

—Michael Easley

role confusion

- Culture has created a "gender blender" when it comes to roles and responsibilities in a marital relationship.
- Someone has to take the lead in a relationship.
- Many couples begin marriage with a 50/50 approach to the relationship.

reasons the 50/50 plan is destined to fail[6]

1) **Acceptance is based on performance.** For many people, performance becomes the glue that holds the relationship together, but it isn't really glue at all. It's more like Velcro. It seems to stick, but it comes apart when a little pressure is applied.

2) **Giving affection is based on merit.** With the "meet me halfway" [50/50] approach, a husband would give affection to his wife only when he felt *she had earned it*. She, in turn, would lavish affection and praise only when she felt *he had earned it*.

3) **Motivation for action is based on feeling.** As a newlywed, it's easy to act sacrificially because the pounding heart and romantic feelings fuel the desire to please. But what happens when those feelings diminish? If you don't feel like doing the right thing, perhaps you won't do it at all.

4) **Rejection is based on focusing on weakness.** One spouse often focuses on how the other spouse is not doing his or her "half." Both constantly fall short of halfway because each person defines the midpoint differently. Ask a husband or wife to list his or her spouse's strengths in one column and the weaknesses in another, and the weaknesses will usually outnumber the strengths five to one.

equal value, different roles

There are many areas in life in which we are called upon to play a role that is different from the role others are playing. It's true at work, at school, at church, in sports, and in community organizations. A football team is a classic example: Each player has a different job, and every job is important. If someone misses an assignment, the quarterback can get his head knocked off! And although he is often paid the most, the quarterback is the first to acknowledge that he could not do his job without the offensive linemen.

The Family Manifesto: FamilyLife created *The Family Manifesto* to provide families with a Scripture-based blueprint for building godly homes. The document supports the conviction that the family is the backbone of the Christian church and of society as a whole. The manifesto, which can be read in its entirety on the FamilyLife website, is a declaration of values to help couples uphold, strengthen, and continue to build upon the biblical institutions of marriage and family.

> ***The Family Manifesto* on marriage:** We believe that God created marriage for the purpose of couples glorifying God as one flesh, parenting godly children, and enjoying sexual pleasure. "As iron sharpens iron" (Proverbs 27:17, NIV), we believe that God uses marriage to sharpen a man and a woman and mold them into the image of Jesus Christ. Just as the Trinity reflects the equal worth of Father, Son, and Spirit, with differing roles, we believe that God created a man and a woman with equal worth but with differing roles and responsibilities in marriage.

"When two people are on a horse, one of them has to be in front."

—Dennis Rainey

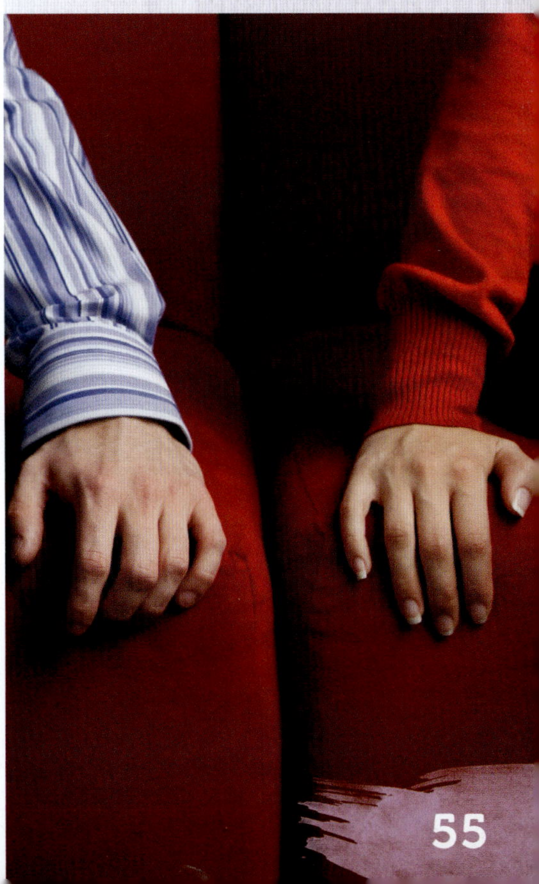

take it to heart

biblical roles in marriage

Read the verses below, and then answer the questions that follow:

Ephesians 5:22–26, 33

22 ***Wives***, *submit to your own husbands, as to the Lord.* 23 *For the*
husband is the head of the wife even as Christ is the head of the
church, his body, and is himself its Savior. 24 *Now as the church*
submits to Christ, so also wives should submit in everything to
their husbands.

25 ***Husbands***, *love your wives, as Christ loved the church and gave*
himself up for her, 26 *that he might sanctify her, having cleansed*
her by the washing of water with the word. . . . 33 *Let each one of*
you love his wife as himself, and let the wife see that she respects
her husband.

1) What is the primary instruction to the wife in this passage?

2) What is the primary instruction to the husband?

3) On a scale of 1 to 10, how would you say you are doing as a couple in fulfilling these roles?

1 2 3 4 5 6 7 8 9 10

NOT WELL AT ALL **VERY WELL**

defining a husband's role

- A husband's privileged role is to love his wife as Christ loved the church.

> *"Husbands, love your wives, as Christ loved the church and gave himself up for her."*
>
> —Ephesians 5:25

- To do this a husband has to know his wife, pay attention to her, nurture her, cherish her.

> *"For no one ever hated his own flesh, but nourishes and cherishes it, just as Christ does the church."*
>
> —Ephesians 5:29

- The husband is called to be the head of his wife, just as Christ is head of the church.

> *"For the husband is the head of the wife even as Christ is the head of the church."*
>
> —Ephesians 5:23

- "Headship" means that the man sacrifices himself—his needs, desires, dreams—for the sake of his family.
- "Headship" also means that the man has the burden of taking the initiative to move things forward on behalf of his family.

> *"My role is to live to make my wife great."*
>
> —Crawford Loritts

According to a Yahoo! HotJobs' survey,[7] some of the qualities for being a good leader (in order of importance) are . . .

1) **Communication and listening skills**
2) **Effective leadership skills**
3) **Trust in their employees to do their job well**
4) **Flexibility and understanding**
5) **Teamwork skills**
6) **Even temperament**
7) **Interest in employee development**
8) **Ability to share credit**

how a husband nourishes and cherishes his wife[8]

by Barbara Rainey

- Seek to understand her role and her struggle.
- If she works outside the home, understand her job and the pressures it places on her, especially regarding her role at home.
- Verbalize often, especially during her times of failure and discouragement, your complete acceptance of her. (Be sure that you really *do* accept her.)
- Liberally verbalize belief in her as a person and in her ability and worth.
- Verbalize your need for her and back it up by sharing with her your fears, failures, needs, dreams, hopes, and discouragements. Do it cautiously if this is new to you.
- Share at times when she can listen attentively and appreciate your transparency. (Don't share something serious when she's preoccupied with the kids or dinner.)
- Notice and praise her for the things she does for you (meals, laundry, etc.).
- Be willing to help her work through difficulties in her life: discipline, problems with the children, relationships with friend and parents, fears, resentment, etc.
- Be patient and realize that nourishing and cherishing is a lifetime process.

the meaning of *kephale* ("head")

Dr. Wayne Grudem, in his effort to defend a biblical view of roles in marriage, sought to inspect every use of the Greek word *kephale*, which is translated "head" in Ephesians 5:23. He found 2,336 occurrences of the word in ancient Greek literature, and in *every* instance, it was used to mean "authority over/ruler." He went on to assert that "no examples have ever been found where person A is called the 'head' of person B and person A is not in a position of authority over person B."[9]

what does it mean for a husband to be the head of his wife?

Many women have a hard time accepting the teaching that the husband is the "head" of the wife because they have witnessed the abuse of this role. Some men, after hearing they are the "head" of their wives, have understood this to mean that a man can order his wife around and treat her like a slave. No man who reads Ephesians 5:23–30 could reasonably come to such a conclusion.

But when a biblical principle is misused, it does not inherently mean that the concept is faulty. The apostle Paul calls a man to lead as Christ leads the church, sacrificially, treating his wife as his own body. He should nourish and cherish her and cleanse her "by the washing of water with the word" (verse 26). The language here is very gentle and caring. No man could truly fulfill his responsibility as the leader of his home without learning to lovingly sacrifice his own life for the sake of his wife.

on your own

What are five ways I could sacrifice more for my wife?

1)

2)

3)

4)

5)

***The Family Manifesto* for husbands:**

We believe God has charged each husband with fulfilling the responsibility of being the "head" (servant leader) of his wife. We believe God created a man incomplete, and as a husband, he needs his wife as his helper. We believe a husband will give account before God for how he has loved, served, and provided for his wife. We reject the notion that a husband is to dominate his wife. Likewise, we reject the notion that a husband is to abdicate his responsibilities to lead his wife. Rather, we believe his responsibility is to love his wife. This love is characterized by taking the initiative to serve her, care for her, and honor her as a gift from God. We believe his responsibility is to protect his wife and help provide for her physical, emotional, and spiritual needs.

We also believe a husband is to seek after and highly regard his wife's opinion and counsel and treat her as the equal partner she is in Christ. Therefore, we are committed to exhort and implore men not to abuse their God-given responsibilities as husbands, but rather to initiate a sacrificial love for their wives in the same way Jesus Christ initiated sacrificial love and demonstrated it fully on the cross (Genesis 2:18–25; Ephesians 5:22–33; Colossians 3:19; 1 Peter 3:7; 1 Timothy 5:8).

wayne and margaret grudem: before phoenix[10]

Wayne Grudem's decision to move to Phoenix, Arizona, for his wife's health was done sacrificially, with deep concern for her needs. Loving her in this way was something he learned [not only] from the Scriptures but also from a mistake he made early in their marriage.

Wayne's first teaching job was at Bethel College in Minneapolis, Minnesota. After almost four years of teaching, he received a call from Trinity Evangelical Divinity School with a job offer.

Wayne said, "Almost immediately I was very interested, because I wanted to train pastors."

Margaret remembers that they discussed it, but she said, "I could tell that his mind was already made up."

They moved to Illinois soon thereafter, but looking back, Wayne says, "I don't think I was very thoughtful of Margaret. . . . She loved it at Bethel, [but] the decision-making process, looking back, wasn't exactly right. And Margaret was hurt by it."

Margaret remembers the hurt: "I felt like I didn't have a voice. I had been helpful and encouraging of Wayne to finish his different degrees, but when we moved to Minnesota, my dad had just died, so I wanted to put down roots, and it felt like a really safe place. And then leaving there and going to Trinity was hard."

Though the move was difficult, Margaret trusted that God was in control of the situation. She said, "I think the Lord wanted Wayne at Trinity, and if I [had] refused to go, I think I would have been disobeying the Lord, and I needed to go ahead and do that with my husband. . . . I think it built character in me and strength in me, and the Lord was really good to us and our kids there."

They eventually met with a counselor to help them work through the hurts, which led Wayne to grow in his love and respect for Margaret: "I think I've grown in my ability to listen to her, and [I have an] immense respect for her wisdom, insight, [and] knowledge of the Lord and the Lord's will." . . . Now, whenever he has any question about his schedule, "the first thing I want to know is her opinion, and then we both pray about it and seek God's help."

twenty-five ways to spiritually lead your family[11]

1) Pray daily with your wife.
2) Write a love letter that she'd like to receive.
3) Discover her top three needs and over the next twelve months go all out to meet them.
4) Buy her a rose. Take her in your arms. Hold her face gently. Look into her eyes and say, "I'd marry you all over again!"
5) Take her on a weekend getaway.
6) Read the Scriptures to her.
7) Replace the "D" word with the "C" word! (D = divorce; C = commitment)
8) Court her.
9) Remain faithful to her.
10) Fulfill your marriage covenant.
11) Have a family time at least one night a week.
12) Use circumstances to teach your children to trust God.
13) Protect your family from evil.
14) Restrain your teenager's passion.
15) Set spiritual goals for your children.
16) Take your children on mission trips.
17) Catch your kids doing something right.
18) Date your daughters.
19) Inspect what you expect.
20) Do a Proverbs breakfast Bible study with your teens (fifteen and older).
21) Hug and kiss your sons and daughters.
22) Ask your children for forgiveness when you fail them.
23) Pray with them.
24) Call them to a spiritual mission to do what God wants to do with their lives.
25) Persevere and don't quit.

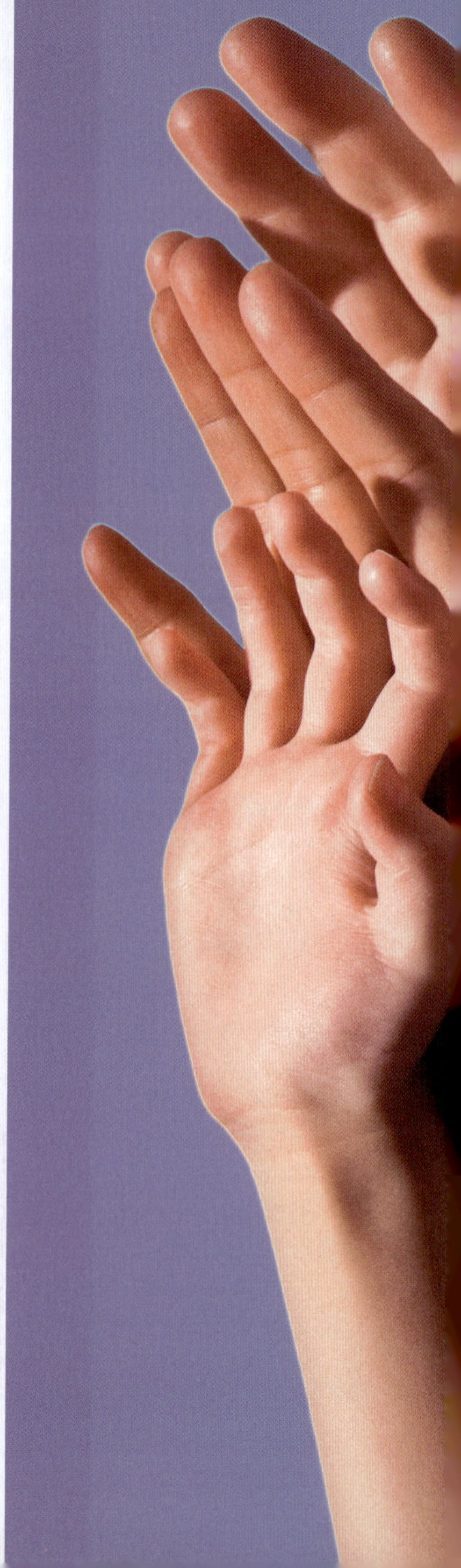

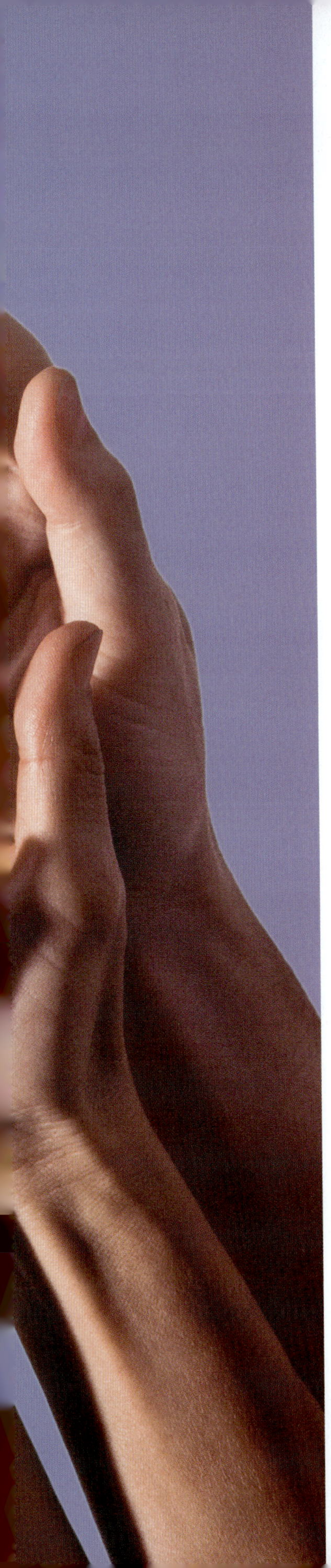

what should a husband do if his wife will not follow his leadership?[12]

- **Maintain an attitude of humility.** Humbly admit that as a man, you still have much to learn about leading your wife.
- **Acknowledge and confess your own sin.** The temptation is to dwell on the sin of your spouse instead of confessing your own.
- **Get in her shoes.** Try to think about the situation from your wife's perspective. Doing so may help you understand why she is struggling to follow your leadership.
- **Know your biblical role.** A husband should memorize and meditate regularly on Ephesians 5:25–33 to remind him of his role.
- **Pray regularly for her.** Pray often that she would come to know and understand God's design for marriage and see your desire to lead her biblically as a good thing.
- **Decide to forgive.** A husband needs to prepare . . . for the inevitable . . . that his wife is going to sin against him and he is going to be tempted to retaliate. Instead of retaliating against your wife, you must choose to forgive, just as you have been forgiven (Ephesians 4:32). This decision will guard against bitterness and allow you to receive your wife graciously, with love.
- **Make God's glory your highest goal.** Learn to be God glorifying, not man centered or wife centered.

  By doing this, the following occurs:

  - If your motive is to glorify God, you will be less vulnerable to intimidation and manipulation.
  - You will be protected from sinful reactions if and when she doesn't respond appropriately to your care, your service, and your leadership. You can be satisfied with and secure in the knowledge that God is pleased with your motive and obedience, regardless of your wife's response, and even experiencing your wife's rejection of your care, service, and leadership.
  - You will be less likely to seek or demand from your wife what only God can provide. You will be satisfied with and by God and will seek to simply serve your wife.

take it to heart

love and lead—a man's role in marriage

Men: In what ways would you like to improve in your role as a husband? Select up to three areas of improvement from the following list:

- ❑ Taking the initiative
- ❑ Leading my wife in a way that makes her feel cherished and understood
- ❑ Verbalizing acceptance and honor to my wife
- ❑ Leading in a way that makes biblical submission easy and reasonable for my wife
- ❑ Showing love for my wife with sacrificial actions
- ❑ Demonstrating love even when I don't feel it
- ❑ Knowing my wife's needs
- ❑ Esteeming my wife in her role as a wife (and a mother)
- ❑ Living with my wife in an understanding way
- ❑ Growing spiritually
- ❑ Making my wife my top priority after God
- ❑ Staying focused on God's plan for me as a husband and father

What one thing can you do in the next week to love and lead your wife better?

Women: List three ways your husband loves and leads you.

what is a woman's role in marriage?

***The Family Manifesto* for wives:**

We believe God has charged each wife to fulfill the responsibility of being her husband's "helper." We believe a wife will give an account to God for how she has loved, respected, and given support to her husband. We uphold the biblical truth that she is of equal value with her husband before God. We reject the notion that a wife should assume the leadership responsibilities of her husband. Likewise, we reject the notion that a wife should passively defer to the dominance of her husband. We believe that her responsibility is to willingly and intelligently affirm, respect, and submit to her husband as the leader in the relationship and in his vocational calling. Therefore, we are committed to exhorting a wife to be in support of her husband by accepting and excelling in her responsibility as his helper (Genesis 2:18–25; Ephesians 5:22–33; Colossians 3:18; 1 Peter 3:1–6; Proverbs 31:10–12).

"The fact that I am a woman does not make me a different kind of Christian, but the fact that I am a Christian does make me a different kind of woman. For I have accepted God's idea of me, and my whole life is an offering back to Him of all that I am, and all that He wants me to be."

—Elisabeth Elliot, *Let Me Be a Woman*

Q&A: a wife's job description[13]

Q: I've heard a lot of differing opinions on a wife's role in marriage. What is a wife's job description? What are the duties and responsibilities involved?

Barbara Rainey: Now, after many years of marriage, I would say that a wife's role in marriage can be summed up in three words: love, support, and respect.

In Titus 2:4, older women are instructed to train the younger women to "love their husbands." Initially that's an easy job, because most of us get married while we're in love. After the feelings fade, though, we have to remember that love is a commitment.

Secondly, we are to support our husbands. Ephesians 5:22 says, "Wives, submit to your husbands as to the Lord." To submit to your husband's leadership is to support his leadership. It means being an encouraging, believing wife who allows her husband to be the leader in the family. It doesn't mean being a doormat. You should share your opinions, your thoughts and feelings, and make decisions together. Ultimately, though, you support your husband's decisions.

Finally, a wife should respect her husband. Ephesians 5:33 commands, "The wife must respect her husband." There are times when that is a hard job; you may not feel that your husband is worthy of respect. However, you are still commanded to respect him. Even if there are many things that he has done wrong, you can find something to respect. Try to remember what you respected about him when you were dating. Does he work hard to financially support the family? Does he play ball with your child?

He may not be doing all that you wish he were doing, but you have to focus positively on the things that he is doing. Verbalize to him your appreciation. When you affirm him and let him know that you value his work, it will be easier for him to continue to lead lovingly.

Proverbs 14:1 says that a "wise woman builds her house, but the foolish tears it down with her own hands" (NASB). As a wife, you have power to create or destroy your relationship with your husband. In your attitude, remember that God is in control, and you can trust him. Also remember that you have to choose to obey God through honoring and obeying your husband. In these ways, you can build a strong house.

defining a wife's role

BEING A HELPER: A woman is called to be a "helper" in the marriage relationship.

- God is called a "helper" in Scripture. If God calls Himself "helper," it shows it is not a derogatory term.

  "From where does my help come? My help comes from the LORD, who made heaven and earth." **–Psalm 121:1–2**

- Helping involves a willing followership, not in a mindless way, but in a vigorous, robust, feminine way that comes alongside a husband as a partner.

RESPECT: Wives are called to respect their husbands (Ephesians 5:33).

- There is no more powerful attitude that a wife can have towards her husband than respect.
- Respect is shown not just with words, but also with actions, and it flows from an attitude of the heart.

  "The wise woman builds her house, but the foolish tears it down with her own hands." **— Proverbs 14:1 (NASB)**

CHEERING HIM ON: Women are called to encourage their husbands to lead their families well.

- For most men, their deepest fear is failure, and their deepest need is the confidence to know they can succeed, the kind of confidence only a wife can provide.
- Even when a husband makes mistakes, he needs encouragement for the ways he is trying to lead.

SUBMITTING: Submission means following leadership.

- The negative tendency in many marriages is for a man to retreat from leadership, and a wife to step in. And while she may be plenty competent to make good decisions, she is still replacing the role that God outlined in the Scriptures.
- Biblical submission does not violate the personality that God has given a woman, but calls her to live out her personality to its fullest, as God intended.

on your own

Wives: What are five ways I can show my husband I respect him?

1)

2)

3)

4)

5)

what is biblical submission?[14]

by Bunny Wilson

- Biblically, *submission* means to yield to people, precepts, and principles that have been placed in our lives by God as an authority.
- Women do not have to submit to anything abusive or immoral. A boss cannot ask her to sign false documents; her husband cannot ask her to sign a false tax return.
- Submission is not an ominous, oppressive force that hangs over a marriage. Rather, it should lead to thoughtful, fruitful discussions about all areas of life.
- Submission is powerful because it operates on pure faith. The act of submitting says, "I believe that God sees all, hears all, knows all, and he will intervene on my behalf."
- A wife cannot say, "I don't have to submit to your final authority if you don't love me as Christ loved the church." She yields to her husband's final decision because that's what God's Word teaches, and she'll learn how power is released when she does that.
- Being submissive can help a husband grow spiritually: "[My husband] said one day in a radio interview . . . , 'When Bunny decided to become submissive, it put the fear of God in my heart, because I knew I was no longer contending with her, I was dealing directly with God.'"
- How does one become submissive? You decide to implement the principle in your life. You choose to submit by faith.
- What if I submit, and my husband makes a mistake? Your husband is not perfect, and there will be times when he makes a bad decision. You could say to him, "I told you so," or you can say, "Anybody can make a mistake. What can I do to help you fix it?" When we forgive a person's mistakes, it bonds them to us, and it makes the relationship even dearer and nearer.

"Women come up to me all the time and say, 'I don't know how I'm going to do this. I'm a strong woman.' God loves strong women. You know why? Because he knows that once we understand a principle and it's clear, we're just as strong toward submission as we were toward rebellion." **—Bunny Wilson**

what if your husband doesn't lead?[15]

1) Don't nag. Love him for who he is. Being nagged at is like being nibbled to death by a duck.
2) Don't plot. Instead, pray for him.
3) Don't look for him to obey God perfectly every time—give him grace and forgiveness.
4) Don't tear him down for who he isn't and what he doesn't do. Build him up, even when you think he doesn't deserve it.
5) Don't listen to ungodly counsel that tells you to quit. Surround yourself with Christians who will encourage you to fulfill your marriage vows.
6) Pray that your spouse will be surrounded by godly Christians who will love him and share with him what he needs to hear. (Don't do it yourself. Let God do it.)

support and respect—a woman's role in marriage

take it to heart

Women: In what ways would you like to improve in your role as a wife? Select up to three areas of improvement from the following list:

- ❑ Showing my husband respect in my attitudes and actions
- ❑ Displaying support for and confidence in him
- ❑ Being content and trusting in God
- ❑ Letting my husband know I admire him
- ❑ Being willing to follow his direction for our home
- ❑ Accepting him regardless of his performance
- ❑ Growing spiritually
- ❑ Making my husband my top priority after God
- ❑ Staying focused on God's plan for me as a wife and mother

What one thing can you do in the next week to respect and support your husband better?

Men: List three ways your wife respects and supports you.

a life of ballet[16]

Dancer Kathy Thibodeaux was the top medalist in the 1982 International Ballet Competition. A year later she left a bright future to start what is now considered the world's foremost Christian ballet company. She says the keys to her long-lasting success have been the strong foundation she received early in her ballet training and consistent rehearsal (usually five hours a day) to keep her skills at the highest level possible.

"What's important about being a dancer is setting a good foundation when you're young. If you don't have that good foundation to build on, you're sure to have problems later on. And in my marriage . . . and in ballet . . . , my real foundation is Jesus Christ."

For almost as long as her thirty-plus-year marriage to Keith (the former Little Ricky on *I Love Lucy*), Kathy has had the same dance partner. For twenty-five years, whenever she has danced duets, it has been with John Vandervelde (who has also been married for more than thirty years to his wife, Karin). John sees many similarities between his role in ballet and as a husband.

"The beauty and elegance the audience sees on the stage is preceded by the bumps and bruises of rehearsal," John says. "It's a lot of effort working the difficulties out before the dance is even presentable. It takes a lot of hard work to bring something from a rough stage to the beauty that people see on stage."

"In pairs dancing as in marriage, there are inevitably going to be errors. There has to be a lot of give and take, forgiveness, and grace. In my marriage to Karin and in my dancing with Kathy, I'm taking the lead for strength [and] support and to provide the sense of confidence that I'm going to be there in every situation."

COMPLETING the Picture

- I will seek to follow God's design, rather than the cultural definition of marriage.
- I choose to honor my spouse as equal in value, and yet to also esteem the way God has designed him or her differently from me.
- **Husbands:** I will strive to lead my wife lovingly and sacrificially.
- **Wives:** I will strive to respect and support my husband.

after the event

Date-Night Ideas

- Head to a place that offers dance lessons for the evening. Do some digging to find out what's available.
- Invest in a six-week class at a local studio, for the two of you.
- Send the kids to a friend or relative, or wait until they turn in for the night; then put on your favorite music and dance in your living room.

Date-Night Discussion

1) What did you find helpful in the video, and in this manual, on the subject of "roles" in marriage?

2) Do you think you have your roles figured out in your marriage?

3) *Husbands, ask your wife:* What can I do to help you feel more loved, respected, and cared for in our marriage?

4) *Wives, ask your husband:* What can I do to help you feel more loved, respected, and supported in our marriage?

5) What do you hope your marriage will look like when you're old? How do you see yourselves treating each other?

Date-Night Prayer

Father of peace, help us to make decisions together and explore our biblical roles further. Help us to figure out how to divide responsibilities and, through it all, show nothing but love toward each other. Amen.

Q&A: making decisions together[17]

Q: In your articles and on radio, you talk about male leadership in the home. But it's also clear that, when you and Barbara are making a decision, you have a lot of interaction with each other. So what happens when Dennis feels strongly one way and Barbara feels strongly another way?

Dennis: First, I think it is clear that the Bible teaches that the husband is responsible for the direction of his home, family, and marriage. And so he is what is called "the head of the house." To me, that means it is my responsibility to go prayerfully before God and with my wife to consider the circumstances and to make a decision. If we can't come to a consensus, it falls upon me to make a decision. And we prefer it that way—if [you] have a "roleless marriage" where there is no final authority, that creates a greater ambiguity.

Barbara: And insecurity too. It seems to me they would be in a state of indecision.

Dennis: In those marriages, it seems that the stronger personality would win regularly.

Q: Do you ever make a decision to go with Barbara's opinion rather than your own?

Dennis: Absolutely. Any good leader knows that you need to gather all the facts and enlist those who may know the situation better than you before you make the decision. In many situations with the children, for example, Barbara will be far more versed and have much more insight into what is going on with the child emotionally and circumstantially. There have been numerous times when we have disagreed and I have asked her to go with me on a decision. But there have been, I would guess, just as many [times] where she has disagreed with me and I have changed my mind and gone with her.

Barbara: You've been real good about deferring to that woman's intuition in our relationship. There have been times when I just can't explain why I feel this is the right thing to do with a child. Unless you feel you have a strong case for another choice, you go with what I'm feeling. That validates me as a woman—that my opinions are worth considering and you are going to listen to them.

Dennis: I think we've developed a good amount of trust over the years as we have discussed so many decisions. We've learned that we need the other's input and advice. She will help me avoid problems, and vice versa.

The one area where I typically have not gone with Barbara's opinion over mine repeatedly is in the area of schedule. She has such a mother's heart in wanting to see our children develop their gifts, and it's easy for her to overcommit them and herself. I've seen the toll that takes on her. On more than one occasion I've urged her not to head in certain directions because of the need to protect our home. I feel part of my responsibility is to spiritually, emotionally, and physically protect my family, not merely from evil but from overscheduling, from busyness, and from activity. A good shepherd doesn't lead any faster than the sheep can follow!

Barbara: We went through a time when I was making a lot of decisions regarding the kids without Dennis because I knew how busy he was. I assumed I was saving him some grief, but as a result I was getting everyone overcommitted. I needed the protection that he offered when we make those decisions together. I'm glad to have him to help make decisions. And to tell me if I am wrong.

project two

This application project has two sections: the individual section and the interaction section. Be sure to leave adequate time to interact as a couple following the individual section. We recommend that you *switch manuals* with your spouse before beginning this project.

Individual Section *30–40 Minutes*

PART ONE

Spend time in prayer:

- **a.** Confess to God any rejection of, withdrawal from, or bitterness toward your spouse and agree with him that this is wrong. Thank God for his forgiveness. "If we confess our sins, He is faithful and righteous to forgive us our sins and to cleanse us from all unrighteousness" (1 John 1:9, NASB).

- **b.** Commit to God to receive your spouse based upon God's integrity and sovereignty. Be sure to put this commitment in your love letter to your spouse (see part 2).

- **c.** Commit to God that you will trust Him with your spouse's differences and weaknesses and love your spouse unconditionally with Christ's love (apart from performance). Be certain you put this commitment in your love letter.

- **d.** Spend time reflecting on your differing roles. In what ways have you seen evidence of God's grace displayed in the way you fulfill your roles? Thank God for these examples in your relationship.

- **e.** Tell God you are willing to let Him change you through your spouse's strengths, as well as his or her weaknesses, differences, and selfishness.

PART TWO

Write out the answers to the following questions in the form of a love letter to your spouse. (Use the space provided on the next two pages.) Make sure you have switched manuals so that you are writing this letter in your spouse's manual.

- **a.** What qualities attracted me the most to you when we first met?
- **b.** How has God used our differences to help complete us and to help me grow?
- **c.** HUSBANDS: Think of an example of how your wife has shown you respect and supported you. Take time to encourage her for her efforts.
- **d.** WIVES: Think of an example of how your husband has loved and led you well. Take time to encourage him for his efforts.
- **e.** HUSBANDS: Reflect on your responsibilities as a husband to love and lead your wife. Express one of the ways you commit to grow in each area moving forward.
- **f.** WIVES: Reflect on your responsibilities as a wife to respect and support your husband. Express one of the ways you commit to grow in each area moving forward.

Interaction Section *15–20 Minutes*

Share your love letter with your spouse.

Setting: Get together with your spouse and complete this section after you finish your love letters. Make sure you are in a location where you feel comfortable talking freely.

Objective: To share your feelings and commitment with each other.

Instructions:

1) Share and discuss your love letters.
2) Express the commitments you made to God during your individual prayer time.
3) Close your time together by praying and taking turns thanking God for each other.

a letter OF Love

session **four**

LOVE *Interrupted*

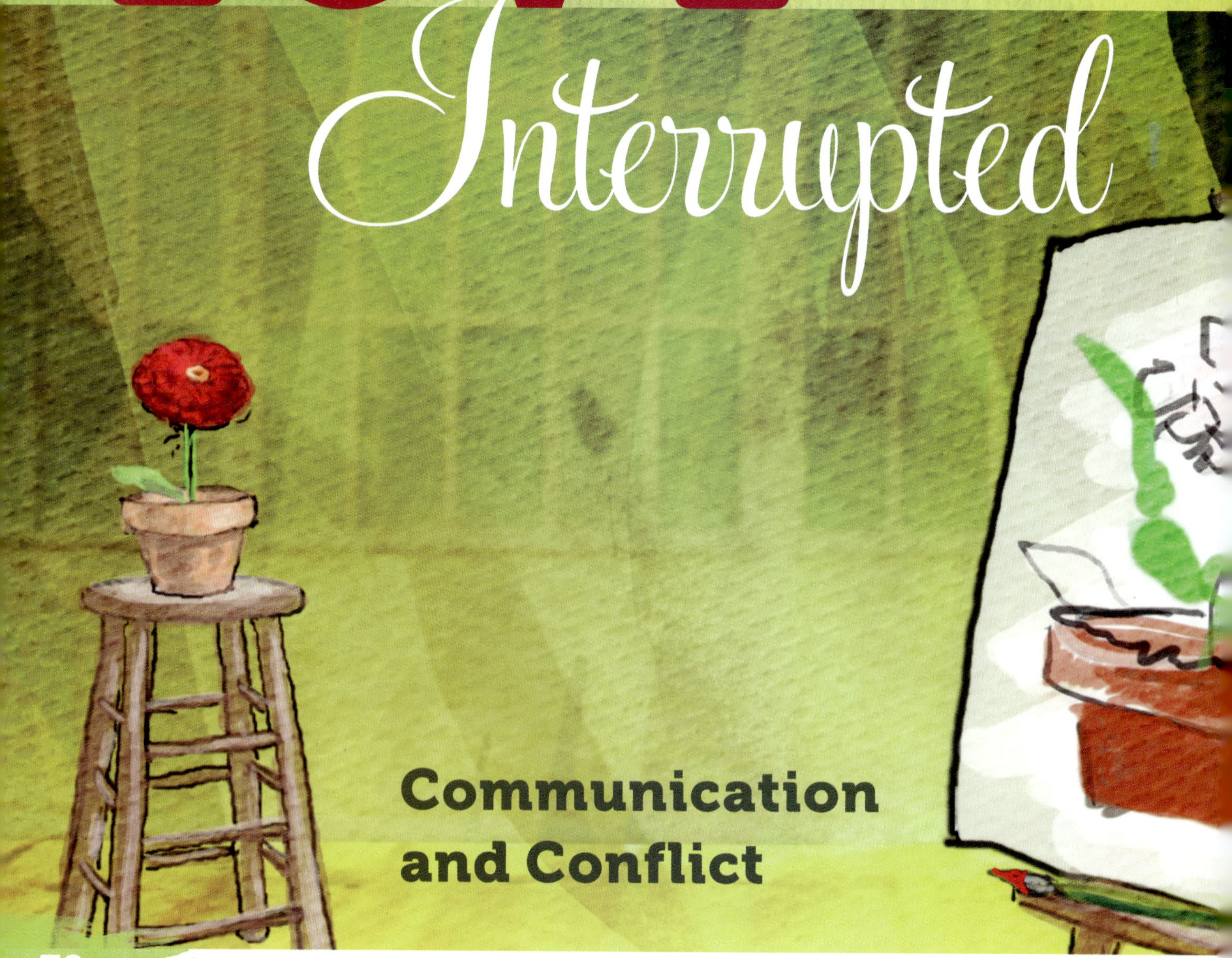

Communication and Conflict

"If you argue and rankle and contradict, you may achieve a victory sometimes; but it will be an empty victory because you will never get your opponent's good will."

—Benjamin Franklin

the BIG brush strokes

- Conflict is common to all marriages.
- The goal is not to be conflict-free but to learn to handle conflict correctly when it occurs.
- Healthy conflict resolution occurs when couples are willing to seek and grant forgiveness.

"I think a lot of people would rather jump out of a moving car than . . . communicate [and] face reality."

—Bobby Conway

tips on communication

- Make sure to address one issue at a time when you're having a conflict.
- To successfully navigate conflict, you need to have the right tools.
- Seek to discover the reason why the conflict began. As you do, you will often find out what is important to your spouse.
- All communication takes place on two levels: the content level (truth) and the relational level (love).

"Rather, speaking the truth in love, we are to grow up in every way into him who is the head, into Christ."

—Ephesians 4:15

- We are often too busy to listen to our spouses and resolve conflict.
- We need to retrain ourselves to be present in the moment with our spouses.

"Let every person be quick to hear, slow to speak, slow to anger . . ."

—James 1:19

handling conflict in your marriage

1) How was conflict handled in your home when you were growing up?

- ❑ Discussed openly
- ❑ Withdrew
- ❑ Attacked
- ❑ Didn't see conflict discussed in our home
- ❑ Given the cold shoulder
- ❑ Pretended nothing happened
- ❑ Talked about it quietly after everyone had calmed down
- ❑ Nagged about it till the other person was finally willing to talk
- ❑ Used snide comments and sarcasm

2) How is conflict handled in your home now?

3) How would you like to improve the way you handle conflict?

dealing with anger

"The anger of man does not produce the righteousness of God." —James 1:20

- The source of our anger is within each of us. No one else can "make us angry."
- Conflict occurs when our desires aren't fulfilled—when we don't get what we want.
    - Our rights have been violated.
    - Our expectations haven't been met.
    - We have been hurt.
- Our unfulfilled desires lead to fighting and quarreling.
- Our unfulfilled desires may result in **ANGER**.

"Anger undealt with kills relationships . . . [and] marriages." —Bryan Loritts

- For conflict to be resolved, both husband and wife must be committed to oneness.

> what causes quarrels AND fights among YOU?
> is it not this, that your PASSIONS ARE AT WAR WITHIN YOU?
> YOU desire and DO NOT HAVE,
> SO YOU murder.
> YOU covet and cannot OBTAIN,
> so you fight and quarrel.
> YOU do not have, because
> YOU do not ask.
>
> James 4:1–2a

more insight

James 4:1—At the source of our quarrels and anger is our "passions." The Greek word used here is also behind our English word for "hedonism," the belief that "pleasure or happiness is the sole or chief good in life."[1] God has wired us to seek pleasure, but pleasure should not be pursued at the expense of obeying Him (Psalm 37:4; 1 Samuel 15:22). To truly get at the source of our "quarrels," one must ask, "Am I pursuing the pleasure of self-fulfillment or pleasure in Christ?"

James 4:2—Murder, fights, and quarrels: three responses to the inner battle of our passions. Murder is the extreme, yet Jesus reminds us that the outward action of murder begins in the heart (Matthew 5:21–22). Quarrels, though not as serious as murder, are often rooted in the same desires for control and manipulation. Efforts to manipulate could often be avoided by simply asking God and our spouse for wisdom regarding our desires. We need to bring our desires before God, genuinely seeking His direction, and "he will give you the desires of your heart" (Psalm 37:4).

Q&A:

Should Children See Parents Argue?[3]

Q: Is it appropriate to resolve conflict in front of younger children?

Barbara Rainey: Many parents set a policy of not arguing in front of their kids. There are some good points about this policy, but I also think it is good for our children to see us disagree and have an argument, as long as we keep those to a minimum and don't frighten the kids or make them feel insecure. Kids learn how to resolve conflict by watching us do it.

tips to cooling off a heated conflict[2]

If you find that small issues tend to quickly escalate into a heated argument in your marriage, then try one of the following tips the next time you're facing a conflict:

- Take a deep breath to stay relaxed.
- Look the other person in the eye, with both of you sitting or standing.
- Speak softly and slowly. ("A soft answer turns away wrath" [Proverbs 15:1].)
- Keep your legs and arms uncrossed. Do not clench your fists or purse your lips.
- Keep reminding yourself: "We *can* find a win-win resolution to this," and remind the other person of this too.
- Watch your language. Words that escalate a conflict are *never, always, unless, can't, won't, don't, should,* and *shouldn't*. Words that de-escalate a conflict are *maybe, perhaps, sometimes, what if, it seems like, I feel, I think,* and *I wonder*. ("So also the tongue is a small member, yet it boasts of great things. How great a forest is set ablaze by such a small fire!" [James 3:5].)
- Affirm and acknowledge the other person's position.
- Ask questions that encourage the other person to look for a solution. Ask open-ended questions rather than ones that will evoke a yes or no response.

confronting in love

- Because we are fallen creatures, we can expect conflict in marriage.
- There are many things in marriage that are not worth fighting about. ("Love covers a multitude of sins" [1 Peter 4:8].)
- However, there are things that, over time, need to be addressed.
- We have a responsibility to lovingly confront when issues are undermining our relationship.

when preparing to confront

- Examine your heart (Matthew 7:4).
- Spend time in prayer.
- Check your motives.
- Choose your timing wisely.

when it's time to confront

- Speak the truth in love (Ephesians 4:15).
- Choose words carefully (Ephesians 4:29).

what to consider when preparing to confront

- Is it worth it? Can I just let it go? ("Good sense makes one slow to anger, and it is his glory to overlook an offense" [Proverbs 19:11].)
- What pattern or habit of mine contributed to the problem?
- Have I spent time praying about this issue?
- Is this the right time to confront?
- What's my motivation? Am I trying to
    - Retaliate—or—Restore?
    - Punish—or—Pursue peace?
- Am I "speaking the truth in love" (Ephesians 4:15)?
- Choose words carefully and with humility. ("Let no corrupting talk come out of your mouths, but only such as is good for building up, as fits the occasion, that it may give grace to those who hear" [Ephesians 4:29].)
- Remember, the goal of loving confrontation is to restore ONENESS in your marriage. ("Brothers, if anyone is caught in any transgression, you who are spiritual should restore him in a spirit of gentleness. Keep watch on yourself, lest you too be tempted" [Galatians 6:1].)

Focus on	Rather than
one issue	many issues
the problem	the person
behavior	character
specifics	generalizations
facts	judgment of motives
"I" statements	"you" statements
understanding	who's winning or losing

focus on . . . rather than . . .

take it to heart

1) In what area from the list on the previous page do you feel you need to improve the most when trying to deal with conflict?

2) Which of the following statements are you more likely to use? (Circle the response that applies for each grouping.)

"You never listen to me!"

—OR—

"I feel like you aren't listening to me."

"You're never around to give me help. I have to take care of the kids by myself, and all you do is watch TV. We never have a chance to talk."

—OR—

"I could really use your help taking care of the baby in the evenings."

"Would you stop being such a slob?"

—OR—

"Could you help me by picking up your dirty clothes in the bedroom?"

"Why do you always criticize me in front of your friends?"

—OR—

"The last time we were with your best friend, I felt hurt when you joked about my clothes."

confronting winston

Winston Churchill, the prime minister of Britain during World War II, was known for his passion and brilliance. His wife, Clementine, wrote the following letter to lovingly confront him about his uncharacteristically harsh treatment of others around him:[4]

My darling . . . I hope you will forgive me if I tell you something that I feel you ought to know. One of the men in your entourage (a devoted friend) has been to me and told me that there is a danger of your being generally disliked by your colleagues and subordinates because of your rough, sarcastic, and overbearing manner. . . . I was astonished and upset, because in all these years I have been accustomed to all those who have worked with and under you, loving you—I said this and was told, "No doubt it's the strain."

My darling Winston, I must confess that I have noticed a deterioration in your manner, and you are not so kind as you used to be.

It is for you to give the orders, and if they are bungled . . . you can sack anyone and everyone. Therefore, with this terrific power, you must combine urbanity, kindness, and if possible, Olympic calm. You used to quote: "One can only reign over souls with calmness." . . . I cannot bear that those who serve the country and yourself should not love you as well as admire and respect you.

Besides, you won't get the best results by irascibility and rudeness. They will breed either dislike or a slave mentality.

Please forgive your loving, devoted, and watchful Clemmie,

[P.S.] I wrote this at Chequers last Sunday, tore it up, but here it is now.

seeking forgiveness

- All Christians have the privilege of seeking and granting forgiveness because of what God has done for them.

  "Be kind to one another, tenderhearted, forgiving one another, as God in Christ forgave you" **(Ephesians 4:32).**

- Some hindrances to seeking forgiveness are
  - lacking time to communicate,
  - being proud in relationships,
  - being too general about the offense, and
  - allowing offenses to pile up.

- When seeking forgiveness
  - begin by admitting to God and yourself that you were wrong.
  - spend time in prayer.
  - be specific.
  - accept responsibility for the consequences.
  - change: consider the attitudes that may have led to the offense and seek to correct them.

steps to seeking forgiveness

- **Be specific:** "I'm sorry for ____________________."
- **Repent:** "I was wrong and don't want to do that again."
- **Ask for forgiveness:** "Will you forgive me?"

Set your spouse free from the debt of the offense. (Don't continue to punish your spouse. Forgive and move on!)

Rebuilding trust is

not automatic;

it takes time, patience,

and grace from God.

granting forgiveness

- True forgiveness is not
  - conditional.
  - forgetting everything that has happened.
  - pretending that something did not happen.
  - an automatic cure for the hurt.
- It is
  - a choice to set your spouse free from the debt of the offense.
  - an attitude of letting go of resentment and vengeance.
  - the first step toward a process of rebuilding trust.
  - an act of obedience to God.

steps to granting forgiveness

1) **Do it privately:** Go to God in prayer.

   God, I forgive ____________________ for hurting me.

2) **Do it publically and specifically:** Go to your spouse and be specific.

   I forgive you for ______________________________.

3) **Do it graciously:** Keep the bigger goal in mind.

   Let's settle this and get on with our relationship.

4) **Do it generously:** Acknowledge your own failings to maintain balance.

   I've done things like that myself.

"God gives you Christ as the foundation of your marriage. 'Welcome one another . . . as Christ has welcomed you, for the glory of God' (Romans 15:7). . . . Don't insist on your rights, don't blame each other, don't judge or condemn each other, don't find fault with each other, but accept each other as you are, and forgive each other every day from the bottom of your hearts."

—**Dietrich Bonhoeffer,** *Letters and Papers from Prison*

For some couples, the idea of actively seeking and granting forgiveness is desired by one spouse and shunned by the other.

Q: How do I pursue peace if my spouse is unwilling?

A: Actively choose to bless your spouse.

Finally, ALL OF YOU, have unity of mind, sympathy, brotherly love, a tender heart, and a humble mind. Do NOT repay EVIL FOR EVIL or REVILING FOR REVILING, but on the contrary, bless, for to this you were called, that you may obtain a blessing. For "whoever desires to LOVE LIFE AND SEE GOOD DAYS, let him keep his tongue FROM EVIL and his lips from SPEAKING DECEIT; LET HIM TURN away FROM EVIL and do good; let him seek peace and pursue it. For the eyes of THE LORD ARE ON THE RIGHTEOUS, and HIS ears are open to their prayer. But the face of the Lord is against those who DO evil."

1 Peter 3:8–12

"When he was reviled, he did not revile in return; when he suffered, he did not threaten, but continued entrusting himself to him who judges justly." —1 Peter 2:23

how to give a blessing

1) Keep your "tongue from evil" and your lips "from speaking deceit" (1 Peter 3:10).
2) "Turn away from evil" (verse 11).
3) "Do good" (verse 11).
4) Keep the goal in mind and "seek peace" (verse 11).

COMPLETING the Picture

- I choose to believe that conflict is common to all marriages.
- I will seek to handle conflict correctly when it occurs in my marriage.
- I will practice seeking and granting forgiveness with my spouse.

after the event

Date-Night Ideas

- Think back to a time when you had the most fun "making up" after an argument. Try to find a creative way to re-create that time together.
- Take a six-week course of kickboxing lessons together. Over a healthy meal afterward, discuss the questions below.
- Light candles and have a picnic in the living room. Sit knee to knee and take turns whispering reasons you love the person sitting in front of you.
- Have a water fight. (Go on! It's fun!) Equal-weapons arsenal and access to water are a must.

Date-Night Discussion

1) What did you find helpful in the video, and in this manual, on the subject of conflict?

2) Each of you answer: The way my parents handled conflict resolution was by . . .

3) Do you think that the model of conflict resolution is or isn't repeated in your marriage? What do you want to do differently?

4) Each of you answer: I think we do/don't have some issues to address in our marriage that are pulling us apart. (They are . . .)

5) What three steps could you take as a couple to resolve the next issue you face (or one you just talked about above)?

Date-Night Prayer

Father of forgiveness, help us to work through any conflict we have, in your name. Remind us how You first forgave us, so we can always forgive each other. Help us to live out Your teachings of mercy, grace, and love. Amen.

controlling your anger[5]

by Crawford Loritts

It was twenty-five years ago, but I still remember the lesson I learned from the near disaster in the Loritts home. My wife, Karen, and I were arguing, and I had become very angry. I felt that she wasn't understanding what I was trying to tell her. We weren't shouting at each other, but the intensity level of the conversation had taken a decidedly upward turn.

I wanted to get out of our apartment to cool off, so I turned to walk out the door. As I did, I passed by our first child, Bryan, a toddler at the time, who was sitting in the middle of the living room floor. I walked out the door and slammed it behind me, and when I did the glass in the door shattered and sprayed around the living room floor.

When I heard the sound of the breaking glass, I felt a wave of panic as I remembered that Bryan was sitting close to the door. I spun around to see that my son was surrounded by shards of glass but that he miraculously was not injured. I can still see him sitting there, jagged pieces of glass sitting mere inches from him.

Crawford, your outburst of anger could have hurt your son very badly, I thought.

I was so grateful that Bryan wasn't hurt by my tantrum. And I was grateful for the lesson this incident taught me. To this day, whenever I am tempted to engage in an outburst of anger, God brings that scene back to my mind. We need to make sure we have control over our anger. Although some Bible teachers and preachers might assert that anger itself is a sin, it is a God-given emotion that has its place in a godly life, as long as it is kept under control. Anger becomes sin when we lose control of it—when it controls us.

This kind of anger—anger that is based on human emotion and not on godly wisdom—is poison to relationships of all kinds. Marriages, friendships, business partnerships, and parent-child relationships suffer and even die when uncontrolled anger is allowed to enter the picture. The apostle James had this to say about anger:

> *This you know, my beloved brethren. But everyone must be quick to hear, slow to speak and slow to anger; for the anger of man does not achieve the righteousness of God.* (James 1:19–20, [NASB])

In other words, you can save yourself a lot of trouble if you keep your ears open, your mouth closed, and your temper under control. We will keep our anger under control when we learn to lend an ear to a situation, then respond appropriately. When we keep quiet and patiently listen to the facts, we keep ourselves from flying off the handle, or reacting in unwarranted and ungodly anger. In short, we must make sure we respond to the facts and avoid reacting emotionally to what we see.

Before you allow yourself to get angry, take a deep breath, count the cost of the anger, submit your anger to the ruling of the Holy Spirit, then respond as He would have you respond. When you do these things, you'll find yourself wasting a lot less valuable time and emotion on useless anger.

project three

This application project has two sections: the individual section and the interaction section. Be sure to leave adequate time to interact as a couple following the individual section.

Individual Section *15 Minutes*

Objective: To practice seeking and granting forgiveness

PART ONE

1) Think of an area in your marriage in which you often find yourselves unable to come to a point of agreement. To assist you, we have listed five areas in which couples regularly experience conflict. You may choose one of these or any other area that applies:

- finances
- intimacy
- children
- in-laws
- roles and responsibilities
- other: ____________________

2) As you review the list above, try to identify one of the following:

a. An unresolved or recurring conflict in which you have hurt your spouse
b. An area of disappointment or hurt in your marriage
c. An area where growth is needed in your marriage

3) In what ways have you contributed to the conflict and the continuing lack of resolution?

4) If you are remarried: What, if any, unhealthy patterns of resolving conflict are you repeating that you exhibited in your previous marriage?

5) Are you willing to move toward reconciliation in this area by asking your spouse to forgive you?

PART TWO

Prepare your heart by humbling yourself before God. Confess any anger that may be keeping a wall up in your marriage and your spouse at a distance. Ask God to reveal to you how you have contributed to the problems in this area of your marriage. Thank Him for forgiving you (1 John 1:8–9). Then acknowledge your willingness before God to seek forgiveness from your spouse. Likewise, prepare your heart to grant forgiveness by thanking God for your spouse.

working it out

"Therefore, confess your sins to one another and pray for one another, that you may be healed. The prayer of a righteous person has great power as it is working." —**James 5:16**

Before beginning your conversation with your spouse, prepare by doing the following:

- Make sure to meet in a place where you are able to talk freely.
- Check your heart to see if you are defensive. Be willing to acknowledge your contribution to any problems.
- Concentrate on only using "I" statements that express your feelings, rather than assigning blame or evaluating intentions (e.g., "I feel like . . ." rather than "You meant to . . .").
- Avoid words like *if, but, maybe, you never,* or *you always.*
- Concentrate on understanding your spouse's point of view instead of convincing him or her of yours.
- Express the truth in love.

Interaction Section *20–30 Minutes*

Objective: To verbally seek forgiveness from or grant it to your spouse

STEP 1 **Husband:** Share with your wife your answers from part 1 of the individual section.

While looking at your wife, restate the issue for which you would like to seek forgiveness, and then ask her forgiveness. (If you find it helpful, follow the example from "Steps to Seeking Forgiveness" on page 89.)

Wife: Grant forgiveness to your husband with your words. Be honest. (If you find it helpful, follow the example from "Steps to Granting Forgiveness" on page 90.)

Then, if appropriate, take the offense, write it on a separate sheet of paper, and throw it away or burn it as a symbolic gesture of the freedom forgiveness grants.

STEP 2 **Wife:** Share with your husband your answers from part 1 of the individual section.

While looking at your husband, restate the issue for which you would like to seek forgiveness, and then ask his forgiveness. (If you find it helpful, follow the example from "Steps to Seeking Forgiveness" on page 89.)

Husband: Grant forgiveness to your wife with your words. Be honest. (If you find it helpful, follow the example from "Steps to Granting Forgiveness" on page 90.)

Then, if appropriate, take the issue, write it on a separate sheet of paper, and throw it away or burn it as a symbolic gesture of the freedom forgiveness grants.

session **five**

LOVE Sizzles

Experiencing Real Intimacy

"Sex is good because the God who created sex is good. And God is glorified greatly when we receive his gift with thanksgiving and enjoy it the way he meant for it to be enjoyed."

—Ben Patterson, in *Sex and the Supremacy of Christ*

the BIG brush strokes

- God created sex and has a wonderful design in mind.
- A satisfying sex life is the result of a satisfying marriage relationship.
- The ultimate purpose of sex is to bring glory to God by celebrating our oneness.

the creation of sex

"God could have designed Adam to subdivide, as an amoeba, but he doesn't."

—Dr. Russell Moore

Did a caveman invent sex? Hardly. Sex is something God designed, and He has an amazing design in mind! A big part of this design is that it occur only in the safety and security of marriage.

Many scoff at this idea, crying foul and saying, "Surely God wouldn't ask us to do the impossible and deny our natural desires." But are we to frolic freely like cavemen, never suppressing the animalistic urge?

Professor David Barash writes in his article "Deflating the Myth of Monogamy,"

"There is no question about monogamy's being natural. It isn't. But at the same time, there is no reason to conclude that adultery is unavoidable, or that it is good. 'Smallpox is natural,' wrote Ogden Nash. 'Vaccine ain't.' Animals, most likely, can't help 'doing what comes naturally.' But humans can. A strong case can even be made that we are never so human as when we behave contrary to our natural inclinations, those most in tune with our biological impulses."[1]

God's design for sex

- The Bible gives *three reasons* for sexual intercourse:

  1) Oneness before God

  2) Pleasure

  3) Procreation

- The ultimate purpose of sex is a celebration of our oneness in the sight of God.
- God created sex and called the union between man and woman "very good" (Genesis 1:31).
- God created sex to be enjoyable, pleasurable, and passionate in marriage.

Let your fountain
be blessed,
and rejoice in the
wife of your youth,
a lovely deer,
a graceful doe.
Let her breasts fill you
at all times with
delight;
be intoxicated
always in her love.

—Proverbs 5:18-19

In the Old Testament, the book of the Song of Solomon captures the romantic relationship between a young man and a young woman. Each of these young lovers writes a letter describing the attributes he or she finds most attractive in the other:

his love letter to her

"[1]How beautiful are your feet in sandals, O noble daughter! Your rounded thighs are like jewels, the work of a master hand. [2]Your navel is a rounded bowl that never lacks mixed wine. Your belly is a heap of wheat, encircled with lilies. [3]Your two breasts are like two fawns, twins of a gazelle. [4]Your neck is like an ivory tower. Your eyes are pools in Heshbon, by the gate of Bath-rabbim. Your nose is like a tower of Lebanon, which looks toward Damascus. [5]Your head crowns you like Carmel, and your flowing locks are like purple; a king is held captive in the tresses. [6]How beautiful and pleasant you are, O loved one, with all your delights! [7]Your stature is like a palm tree, and your breasts are like its clusters. [8]I say I will climb the palm tree and lay hold of its fruit. Oh may your breasts be like clusters of the vine, and the scent of your breath like apples, [9]and your mouth like the best wine." **—Song of Solomon 7:1–9**

nose like a tower of lebanon?

Nothing is more romantic than having your pronounced snout praised or your big belly blessed, right? Well, maybe not. Not having been born in ancient Israel, modern readers find that the meaning of some of these love-letter lines are lost on them. Here is a brief explanation of a few of the trickier sayings:

WHAT IT SAYS	WHAT IT MEANS TODAY
"Eyes are like doves beside streams of water" (5:12)	His eyes are healthy and white, and apparently, the man doesn't mind shedding a tear.
"Cheeks are like beds of spices" (5:13)	His beard smells good enough to kiss!
"Navel is a rounded bowl" (7:2)	She is a dream come true, like a cup of wine that never empties.
"Belly is a heap of wheat" (7:2)	Her skin is a lovely golden brown; it is as beautiful as the flowers of the field.
"Nose is like a tower of Lebanon" (7:4)	Her face is as beautiful as the most majestic mountain in Israel.

her love letter to him

"10 My beloved is radiant and ruddy, distinguished among ten thousand. 11 His head is the finest gold; his locks are wavy, black as a raven. 12 His eyes are like doves beside streams of water, bathed in milk, sitting beside a full pool. 13 His cheeks are like beds of spices, mounds of sweet-smelling herbs. His lips are lilies, dripping liquid myrrh. 14 His arms are rods of gold, set with jewels. His body is polished ivory, bedecked with sapphires. 15 His legs are alabaster columns, set on bases of gold. His appearance is like Lebanon, choice as the cedars. 16 His mouth is most sweet, and he is altogether desirable. This is my beloved and this is my friend, O daughters of Jerusalem." —Song of Solomon 5:10–16

allegorical or literal?

A number of famous people in the history of the church have thought that the Song of Solomon was written as an allegory about Christ's love for the church. Pastor C. J. Mahaney offers a few reasons why we should think otherwise:[2]

1) It is obviously about sex: "Just consider all the sensual and erotic language in the book!"
2) "The Bible never suggests that this book isn't primarily about sex."
3) God's relationship with man is never portrayed as sexual in the Bible.
4) "Spiritualizing the book doesn't work." Some of the statements become very strange if you try to view them symbolically.
5) We should expect to find God giving us guidance in the Scriptures about such an important topic as sex!

song of solomon and sex

- God intended for us to explore our sexuality within marriage—it's a gift.
- We're not to put sexuality in a box; there's a liberty for creativity, initiative, and pursuit.
- The Song of Solomon is in the Bible to inspire married couples as to what could be.
- A goal of sexual intimacy is to see that your spouse has a wonderful, safe, lovely, profound, and fulfilling experience, and to enjoy your relationship with each other around that experience.
- Sex is not to be given only as a favor or seen as an entitlement.
- We must learn to communicate our expectations for sex with our spouse.
- Sometimes we have to save energy to reserve it for sexual fulfillment.

rate your romance

Husbands and wives often have different expectations and desires related to sexual intimacy. Which of the following areas do you think your spouse would identify as a key area that needs to be addressed in your marriage?

- ❑ How often we have sex
- ❑ The timing of when we choose to have sex
- ❑ Our emotional connectedness
- ❑ Time spent together outside the bedroom
- ❑ Time spent in foreplay before having sex
- ❑ How we verbalize and/or display our affection and love
- ❑ The amount of nonsexual touch we share
- ❑ The strength of our relationship with God

What one step can you take this week to address this area?

"Sin corrupts everything . . . [and] it drives couples apart in their physical relationship." —Dave Harvey

"Sexual intimacy doesn't happen automatically. . . . It means getting to know one's husband or wife, which often takes a long time." —Russell Moore

communicating about sex

For some, talking about sex can be awkward or uncomfortable, especially if there have been some bumps in the road in the relationship. But husbands and wives should find freedom and joy in learning to talk openly about likes and dislikes between the sheets. Here are a few ideas for communicating about sex:

- **Pray.** If you are anxious about discussing sex, then spend some time praying for wisdom and for God to soften the heart of your spouse. Pray that God would also help your heart to be in the right place before you approach your spouse.
- **Wait for the right moment.** As in humor, timing is everything in communication. When talking about sensitive subjects, finding the right location and time will help defuse some of the obstacles to good communication.
- **Be clear about your likes and dislikes.** Your spouse cannot read your mind, so if there is something he or she does sexually that you like, make sure to let your spouse know! And though it's more difficult to mention, your spouse needs to know about the turn-offs as well. Your spouse wants to please you in the bedroom, so help him or her know how to do a great job.
- **Use good communication principles.** Avoid using words like "You always . . ." or "You never . . . ," or being accusatory in your tone. Instead, assume the best about your spouse's intentions and desires and use phrases like "I feel like . . ." and "Help me understand. . . ."
- **Learn to flirt!** It is okay to lighten the mood a bit by flirting with each other outside of the bedroom. Discreetly mentioning your desires can help build excitement and anticipation for the big moment.

issues with intimacy

Even if you can talk openly about your sexual relationship, some couples still face challenges in the bedroom because of other issues. Following are the eight most frequent problems couples deal with, along with some ideas and resources for working through these issues.

Challenges to Sexual Intimacy

1) Past Sexual History

There is a cultural myth that having sex before marriage has very little, if any, bearing on your sex life after marriage. But in reality, many married couples deal with guilt and shame from past decisions. Here are a couple of books we recommend if you're struggling with similar issues:

Reclaiming Intimacy by Heather Jamison—Heather shares her personal experience with the counterfeit intimacy of premarital sex in college that led to guilt and resentment. The result was a broken marriage that brought about repentance, forgiveness, and eventual restoration. Her story will help you find joy in reclaiming intimacy in your marriage and the hope and holiness of the Christian life.

The Invisible Bond: How to Break Free from Your Sexual Past by Barbara Wilson—God designed sex to be a powerful and unifying bond. But outside of marriage, the bonds of sex can be devastating. Long after the lover is gone, the bond remains, negatively impacting our lives and future relationships. This book shows you not only how to break those bonds, but also how to embrace a new, abandoned, wise, and thankful heart.

Romans 8:1 reminds us that there is "no condemnation for those who are in Christ Jesus." Those who are in Christ can be set free from the guilt and condemnation of their past because they are now new creations in him.

2) Other Priorities

Except for during the honeymoon, life involves other priorities than just having sex. Distractions, kids, jobs, clubs, meetings, sports, home and auto repairs, yard work, extended family needs, (and dirty kitchens?)—the list of things that demand our attention goes on and on. All these demands add stress to a marriage, which doesn't help either! Between the exhaustion of a long day at work and a bunch of curious, rambunctious children in the home, some couples find it a challenge to even have time for sex. If this describes your love life, here's one book that can renew your passion:

> ***Rekindling the Romance***—Dennis and Barbara Rainey have written this book to help couples reignite the spark in their relationship. This resource helps couples understand their differences and learn to pursue each other in fresh, new ways.

3) Children

Q: How do you handle it when your child wants to invade your time with your spouse?[3]

Dennis Rainey: "Many years ago I determined that there was only one way Barbara and I could emerge intact from having six kids in ten years, and that was to protect our time as a couple. That means setting priorities that discriminate in favor of your marriage rather than against it.

"In addition to regularly scheduled date nights, on certain evenings we close the door to our room and say to our kids, 'If this door is shut, don't come in. Mom and Dad need quiet time together.' Now, we could tell when a child really needed us, but generally we held to this rule. Moms and dads need time to relate and talk to each other. The kids need to know that their parents' marriage relationship is a priority."

Barbara Rainey: "It's especially important to schedule date nights with your spouse when your kids are younger than eleven or twelve. When they move into the adolescent years, it's more difficult to carve out time together because your kids are staying up later at night. If you're not in the habit of spending time together as a couple, you'll really find it hard when your kids enter the teenage years. You need to establish that pattern early on."

Make sure to read chapter 9 in *Rekindling the Romance* to learn more about dealing with the "little interruptions" that can interfere with romance.

4) Pornography

- Thirty-eight percent of adults believe there is nothing wrong with pornography use.[4]
- A 2006 survey found that 50 percent of all Christian men and 20 percent of all Christian women are addicted to pornography.[5]
- Forty-two percent of surveyed adults indicated that their partner's use of pornography made them feel insecure.[6]
- More than half of those engaged in cybersex lost interest in sexual intercourse, and one-third of their partners lost interest as well.[7]
- Up to one in three college men now reports erectile dysfunction, largely due to their overuse of pornography.[8]

Pornography twists and perverts the beauty and the biblical design of God's creation. It leads men and women to look at each other as nothing more than objects of personal pleasure. It causes them to fantasize about sexual relationships with other people, and that's a terrible blow to marital commitment.[9]

If you want to break free from the sexual sin and lust fueled by pornography and romantic fantasies, the first thing you need to realize is that you can't do it in your own power. You need the presence of God in your life, you need accountability relationships, and you need help from experts, even if just in book form.[10]

Accountability—Making friends aware of your struggle with pornography will help you set protective boundaries in your life. One of the most important areas to protect is your computer. Covenant Eyes (www.covenanteyes.com) is a program that monitors your Web use and reports your Internet traffic to an accountability partner of your choice.

Setting Captives Free (www.settingcaptivesfree.com) is a sixty-day, interactive online program that offers help for overcoming addictions of all types.

In *Undefiled*, author Harry Schaumburg discusses how to find freedom from sexual impurity and bring healing to relationships.

5) Misinformation and Misconceptions

Everyone grows up with certain ideas about sex—some are based on reality, but many are based on fiction from movies, TV, magazines, music, and uninformed friends. Getting the right information about sex can help a couple get on the same page and make decisions together. It will also help you talk more about your desires and differences. The following resource is a reliable, biblically based guide to understanding sex:

Sexual Intimacy in Marriage—Dr. William Cutrer has written this book to help couples learn about the way God designed their minds and bodies for sexual intimacy.

6) Abuse

- Approximately one in four girls and one in six boys experience at least one instance of sexual abuse before the age of eighteen.[11]
- Ninety-three percent of juvenile sexual-assault victims know their attacker.[12]
- Victims of sexual assault are more likely to suffer from depression, abuse alcohol and drugs, and contemplate suicide.[13]

Past sexual abuse can be a significant hindrance to intimacy. A painful memory can be triggered at the most unexpected time and completely ruin a romantic moment with your spouse. If you or your spouse has suffered past abuse, the following resource may be of help:

> ***The Wounded Heart*** by Dan Allender offers hope and healing for adults who have been victims of childhood sexual abuse.

7) Romantic Fantasies

Many women engage in romantic fantasies fueled by romance novels, movies, TV shows, and magazines. These are often just forms of pornography that create an unrealistic picture of romance and cause women to become dissatisfied with their husbands. The following book is for women who struggle in this area:

> In ***Every Woman's Battle***, Shannon Ethridge points out that affairs begin not with the first forbidden touch but with the first forbidden thought. Unexpectedly, a woman finds herself enjoying a powerful emotional bond with another man. This book will help you survive the intense struggle for sexual integrity by guarding not just your body but your mind as well.

8) Physical Issues

"[According to Pfizer,] around half of Viagra takers don't refill their prescriptions. . . . Is it because of side-effects? Is it because it's just not working for men with real sexual performance anxiety and erectile problems that a quick fix blue pill just can't fix? Maybe it's just that Viagra can't solve the underlying problems which are the real reason for the male sexual performance anxiety in the first place and, ultimately, never will. . . . Studies have shown that women would rather work on their problems with their partner, open up lines of communication and [improve] their mental, physical and emotional intimacy with one another."[14]

how important is an orgasm?

Dr. William Cutrer, in his book *Sexual Intimacy in Marriage*, addresses this question:

> "No man has ever asked me this. But some women really don't find reaching climax worth the effort required—at least not always. . . . Other women may be unable to reach orgasm because of anatomic reasons, or they may have reached it at times but feel content with sex without orgasm. Some husbands pressure their wives to climax. At this point, it's time to reveal an important principle: whether or not she wants to try to achieve an orgasm is her decision. He must let her decide for herself when she's satisfied. . . . While it's important to satisfy your partner, your partner has the privilege and joy of determining when his or her own satisfaction is achieved.
>
> "Not every intimate encounter must by necessity end with an orgasm. Remember . . . only 25 percent of women experience orgasm whenever they make love. The added pressure to achieve multiple orgasms and/or simultaneous orgasm sets up a standard of success that guarantees frustration and failure for most people most of the time.
>
> ". . . In a giving sexual relationship, both partners will take differences into account. The kind husband will not put pressure on his wife to climax because it may be more enjoyable for her not to have one. Yet if she would like to, he should provide the additional time and effort required.
>
> "Again, statistics are only numbers. You are you. Learn what works best for the two of you and enjoy the journey of sharing life together."[15]

Cutrer goes on to point out that the greater priority for women is generally not reaching a physical climax, but rather, the goal of sex is an emotional and relational connection with their husbands.

> "The priority in intimacy for most women turns out to be something other than physical release:
>
> - 80% would rather have physical closeness
> - 70% would rather have emotional closeness
> - 53% would rather have time together
> - 40% desire physical release"[16]

For more information on this topic, read chapter 8 of *Sexual Intimacy in Marriage*, titled "Questions About Orgasm."

true intimacy

"I'm convinced that for most couples, you fix sexual dysfunction outside of the marriage bed." —Paul David Tripp

- Sexual problems are generally a symptom of another problem.
- Sex is like a thermometer in marriage, not a thermostat, in that it measures the health of your intimacy rather than sets it.
- True intimacy happens when you open up areas of your life to your spouse that are not readily available to others.

Sex is like a thermometer . . . it is primarily a by-product of your relational intimacy.

If there is selfishness, irritation, and frustration in your marriage, these things will come into your marriage bed as well.

why sex is so important to your wife[17]

- Physical intimacy and romance cultivates emotional intimacy with your wife and gives her a sense of security and stability in your relationship and for her as a woman.

- When a man shows sexual interest in his wife, she feels pursued and desired. But when romance, tenderness, and sex are not shared, a sense of loneliness sets in that can ultimately result in emotional and sexual temptation.

- For most men who lack sexual desire, the primary problem is not inadequate interest or erectile dysfunction; it is often a dysfunction of the heart—anger, resentment, and bitterness. Leaving these issues unresolved will lead to further isolation in a marriage.

- A lack of sexual desire for your wife could also be a symptom of a rejection at an earlier point in your marriage. The lingering hurt and thought of being rejected again may seem too great to overcome. You may be withdrawing from her sexually as a strategy to protect yourself. If so, take a step out of the shadows of isolation and into healing with the One who gives "every good and perfect gift" (James 1:17).

why sex is so important to your husband[18]

- Sexual intimacy with your husband gives both of you the comfort of being known and accepted on a deep level that is unlike any other human relationship.
- A man's sexuality, the very essence of his manhood, is primarily expressed through sexual intercourse.
- Temptation can get a foothold when your husband's sexual needs (including the need to feel desired by his wife) remain unmet (1 Corinthians 7:5).
- Safety and security result when we experience being "naked and not ashamed" as did Adam and Eve (Genesis 2:25).

A SATISFYING SEX LIFE IS BUILT

COMMITMENT

FAITHFULNESS	RESPECT	FORGIVENESS
regularly reaffirm your commitment	be a good listener	keep short accounts with each other
build or rebuild trust	validate each other's perspectives and opinions	choose to live in the power of blessing
develop a healthy attitude toward your spouse	never condescend or talk down to each other	remember: "love covers a multitude of sins" (1 Peter 4:8)
develop a healthy attitude toward sex		

WHEN COMMITMENT IS LACKING, SEX CAN SEEM RISKY AND CAN LEAVE A SPOUSE FEELING VULNERABLE.

PASSION

PLANNING	CREATIVITY
make it a priority	enhance the setting
schedule it for the best part of your day	vary the approach

WHEN PASSION IS LACKING, SEX CAN BECOME ROUTINE AND STALE.

ON A FOUNDATION OF . . .

COMPANIONSHIP

COMMUNICATION	TENDERNESS	SPENDING TIME TOGETHER
share openly *listen carefully*	*give creative expressions of affection* *show your love through nonsexual touch*	*share mutual interests* *revive the lost art of dating*

WHEN COMPANIONSHIP IS LACKING, SEX OFTEN LOSES ITS DEPTH.

SPIRITUAL INTIMACY

PRAYER	THE BIBLE
pray together as a couple *pray for each other regularly*	*spend time reading the Bible together* *find verses or passages you can memorize together*

WHEN SPIRITUAL INTIMACY IS LACKING,
SEX CAN BECOME SHALLOW AND SELF-FOCUSED.

making love work

take it to heart

1) Of the four elements of intimacy, which would you like to see strengthened in your marriage?

- ❑ Commitment
- ❑ Companionship
- ❑ Passion
- ❑ Spiritual intimacy

2) What one thing could you do in the next week to strengthen romance and intimacy in your marriage?

COMPLETING the Picture

- I will seek to follow God's design for sex.
- I commit to working through the issues that may be inhibiting a fully satisfying sexual relationship in our marriage.
- To pursue a satisfying sex life, I will also make the overall health of our marriage a higher priority.

after the event

Date-Night Ideas

- Go to the most romantic restaurant in town.
- Pack a romantic picnic full of finger foods you can feed each other—tea-sized sandwiches, bite-sized quiche, chocolate-covered strawberries, glasses for a beverage of choice.
- Ask your husband to describe the perfect afternoon or evening that would get him "in the mood," and then do your best to create it "to order."
- Ask your wife to describe the perfect afternoon or evening that would get her "in the mood," and then do your best to create it "to order."
- Watch a romantic movie together.

Date-Night Discussion

1) What did you find helpful in the video, and in this manual, on the subject of sex?

2) Each of you answer: In your opinion, what is the number-one obstacle to our having a healthy, happy sex life? Is it something we can work through on our own, or do we need to seek a counselor's help?

3) Each of you answer: What physical part of me do you find most attractive?

4) Each of you answer: What would make you think about making love tonight (words, actions, etc.)?

5) Out of the "top ten of all time," describe what you think made your best sexual experience "the best." What factors came together to make it so good? How can you repeat that experience?

6) What about your sex life reflects God's glory? What doesn't?

Date-Night Prayer

Creator, You made us man and woman. Help us to connect in all ways in our marriage—spiritually, mentally, emotionally, and physically. Help us discover greater and greater intimacy and satisfaction in each other. Amen.

three tips for investing in your husband[19]

by Barbara Rainey

The book of Proverbs is probably my favorite in the Bible because it contains such practical wisdom about everyday life. One of its main themes is the value of **developing understanding**.

Consider each of these verses on understanding:

- *[Incline] your heart to understanding* (Proverbs 2:2).
- *Understanding will watch over you* (2:11, NASB).
- *Call understanding your intimate friend* (7:4, NASB).
- *A man [or woman] of understanding walks straight* (15:21).
- *Understanding is a fountain of life to one who has it* (16:22, NASB).

At a Weekend to Remember® marriage getaway I talked to more than a dozen women who were experiencing problems in their marriages. One woman resented her husband's schedule. Another disagreed with her husband regarding how to discipline their children. A third was a young woman whose [spouse] was jealous of the time she spent with her sister.

My advice to these women was basically the same: **Seek to understand** your husband. Focus on him, not on the negative circumstances and how you are affected. Also, give him your complete acceptance, even if you don't totally understand him.

Why is acceptance so important to a man? Because without it, he will feel that you are pressuring him to become something he's not. With it, he will sense that you love him for who he is today and not for what you hope he will become.

The following are three key areas where a woman needs to learn to understand her husband:

Understanding His Need for Work

Man was given the responsibility by God to toil, sweat, and gain from the labor of his hands. His work gives him a sense of significance and importance in the world as he sees his efforts affecting life for good in the present and the future.

But this drive for significance sometimes pushes a man to extremes. Attempting to gain importance through wealth or position, he makes his work his god.

On the other hand, losing a job is a traumatic blow to a man's esteem. It strikes at the core of his dignity. Your husband needs you to help him keep these two extremes in balance. He needs you to praise him for his work, but not to push him to gain too much too quickly. When a man loses or quits his job, his self-esteem can sink. During these times, he needs you to stand beside him and encourage his efforts at finding employment. Men need to work.

Understanding His Sexual Needs

Another sphere in which we wives, for the most part, do not really understand our husbands is in how their self-image is vitally linked to their sexuality. Sometimes we women judge our husbands' sexual needs by our own.

Many wives express that they are offended because their husbands are such sexual creatures. This attitude communicates rejection to a man. To ignore his sexual needs, to resist his initiation of sex, or merely to tolerate his advances is to tear at the heart of his self-esteem.

Jill Renich points this out in her book, *To Have and to Hold.* She states that for a man, "Sex is the most meaningful demonstration of love and self-worth. It is a part of his own deepest person." Thus, a man who feels like a failure in the marriage bed will seldom have the deep, abiding self-respect for which he longs. But, "To receive him with joy, and to share sexual pleasure, builds into him a sense of being worthy, desirable, and acceptable."[20]

What if, on the other hand, your husband expresses little sexual need? Are you naively content because that means less risk for you? Or are you accepting or even resentful of his indifference without seeking to understand why?

Your husband may lack interest in his sexual relationship with you for one of several reasons:

- He may be too busy. Many workaholics have nothing left over for home.
- He may be burying his sex drive, along with many other emotions. He may be experiencing depression, which takes away other basic drives as well.
- He may be deeply afraid of further rejection if you have in any way communicated rejection in the past.
- Unfortunately, he may be involved with another woman.

Women are generally security-minded, but too often a woman's need for security leads her into a sexual rut. Her husband may not say much, so she assumes that he is satisfied too. But he may not be. Beware of complacency. Be willing to make some personal sacrifices to protect your marriage.

As you spend time together physically, be sure to reassure your husband verbally of your unconditional acceptance of him, especially if he is insecure in this area. Tell him that you like his body and that his imperfections and mistakes don't matter to you. His confidence will grow if you allow him the freedom to be himself and to be imperfect.

Understanding His Need for Respect

Part of God's specific instruction to wives is found in Ephesians 5:33: "Let the wife see to it that she respects her husband." In the *Amplified Bible*, this verse reads, "And let the wife see that she respects and reverences her husband—that she notices him, regards him, honors him, prefers him, venerates and esteems him; and that she defers to him, praises him, and loves and admires him exceedingly."

I believe that God, as the designer of men, knew that they would be built up as they are respected by their wives. When a wife respects her husband, he feels it, is supported by it, and is strengthened from it.

Perhaps you are thinking, *But I see little, if anything, to respect.* Perhaps you are like the young mother I know whose husband drank heavily and spent little time with the children. A deliberate change of focus from his weaknesses to his strengths enabled her to begin to see her [spouse] in a positive light. Gaining a better perspective may aid you in esteeming your husband too.

Philippians 4:8 (NASB) tells us: "Whatever is true, whatever is honorable, whatever is right, whatever is pure, whatever is lovely, whatever is of good repute, if there is any excellence and if anything worthy of praise, dwell on these things." Pay attention to your husband's admirable qualities rather than the negative ones. Be patient with him. Keep your hope in God, not in your man. Then you will not be disappointed.

session **six**

LOVE *Always*

Leaving a Lasting Legacy

"Marriage is more than your love for each other. It has a higher dignity and power, for it is God's holy institution through which God wishes to preserve humanity until the end of time. In your love you see only each other in the world; in marriage you are a link in the chain of generations that God, for the sake of [his] glory, allows to rise and fade away, and calls into [his] kingdom." —Dietrich Bonhoeffer, *Letters and Papers from Prison*

the BIG brush strokes

- To leave a godly legacy, we must think about the impact of our lives on future generations.
- Our hope for leaving a lasting legacy is through the gospel of Jesus Christ.
- Leaving a godly legacy requires putting a stake in the ground.

Ten Ideas: Helping Your Marriage Last a Lifetime[1]

The following ten ideas, shared by couples married for fifty years or more, will help your marriage last a lifetime.

1) **You need a Savior.** "We didn't realize that it was two sinners who married each other. Two very sinful people who needed a Savior." (Mona Sproull)

2) **Stay committed to one another.** "Love is not a feeling, it's a commitment . . . no matter what, I will stand by [my wife]." (Charles Powell)

3) **Pray with your spouse.** "Rather than each of us having ourselves at the center of our thinking, there enters a willingness to let God be at the center." (Jerry Bell)

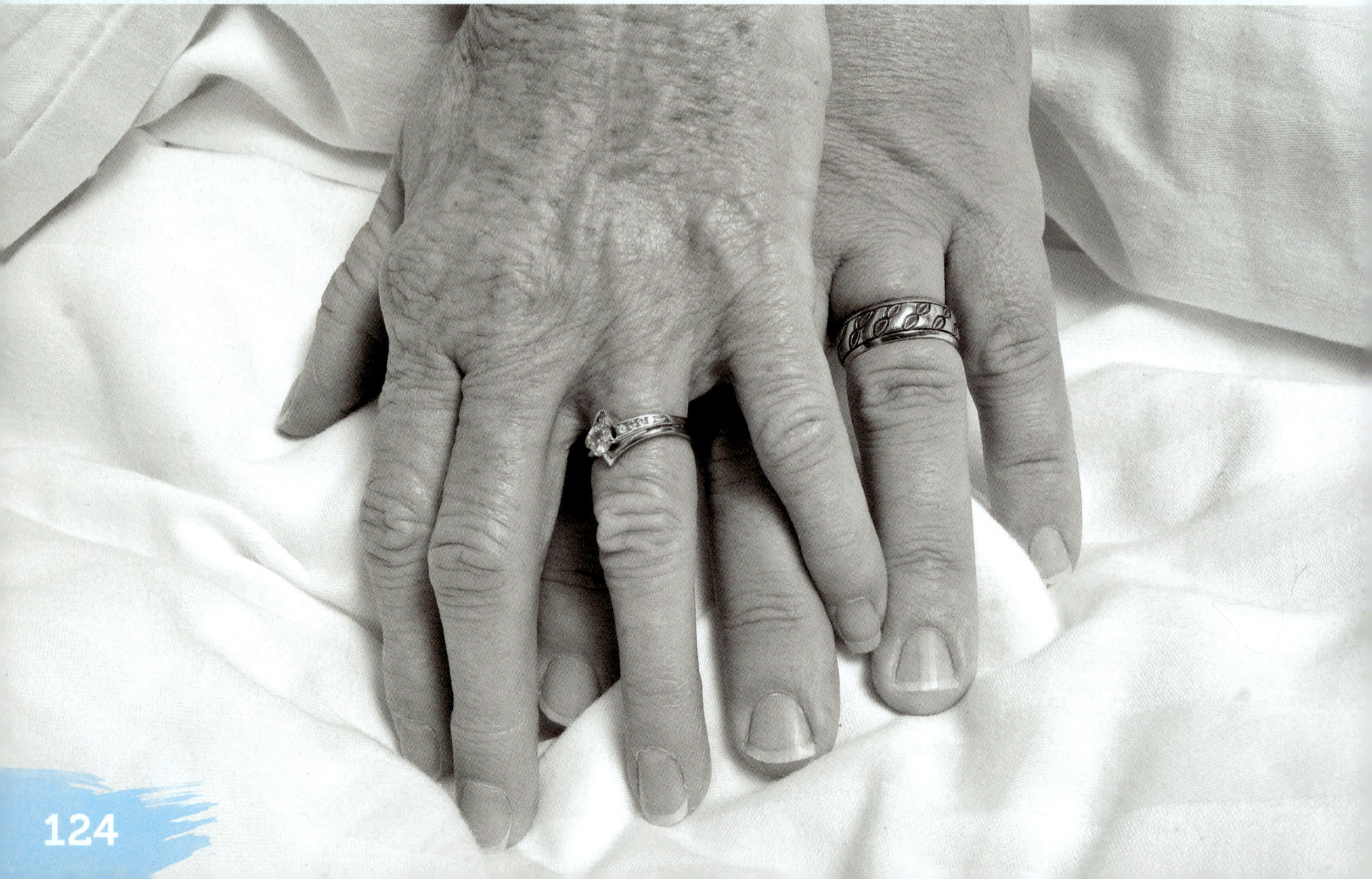

4) **Forgive one another.** "All I could think of was if God could forgive me of all of my sins, who am I not to forgive my husband[?]" (Joan Fortin)

5) **Realize that there's no such thing as a perfect husband or perfect wife.** "Christ has given me understanding and lets me know that everyone does something wrong sometimes." (Mattie Foy)

6) **Have faith that God knows what [He] is doing.** "A lot of people would ask me, 'No children yet?' And I'd say, 'No, but I am sure having a good time telling you how to raise yours.'" (Jodie May)

7) **Trust that God gives grace and direction as you trust [Him].** "How can [parents] trust the Lord when they lose a child? It takes a lot of faith." (Richard Long)

8) **You'll need to make compromises.** "You can't always have your way. I just thought that marriage would be a give and take situation." (Nelda Davenport)

9) **Be objective and take the emotion out of problem solving.** "If I say something to you that's disrespectful to you and I don't really know it, you need to trust my heart." (Mona Sproull)

10) **Love your spouse.** "The love comes from God." (Mattie Foy)

putting a stake in the ground of a new legacy

Jim Whitmore wanted to leave a different legacy than his father left him. Born the only son of "Chip" Whitmore, Jim watched his father cycle through fifteen marriages over the course of his life. "Dad was a real charming guy," Jim recalls. "He could talk a woman into marriage, but he found it easier to resolve conflict by walking away. I knew I never wanted that."

Jim eventually married, but five years later, he found himself on the receiving end of an unwanted divorce. He feared that he was headed down the same path as his father. "The first stake in the ground for me was to admit to God that I had messed up, and that I didn't understand his plan. You can be committed to something, but if you don't have a plan, it doesn't matter. I didn't know God's design."

It was after Jim started working at FamilyLife that he began to learn more about God's plan for marriage. It was there that he also met and fell in love with Karen, a woman he hoped would someday be his wife.

One day they were both attending a staff meeting where Dennis Rainey was speaking about the importance of leaving a godly legacy for future generations. "I wasn't prepared to ask Karen to marry me that day," Jim says. "I didn't even have a ring! I doubted my ability to really be the kind of God-fearing husband Karen needed and to be successful at marriage. But Dennis was speaking on the importance of leaving a legacy for future generations, and I was inspired to say, 'I can begin that legacy today—things can change TODAY.'

"I realized that the best way to put a stake in the ground for our legacy together was to make a public declaration that things would be different. So I went up onstage and asked Karen to marry me that day. Thankfully, she said yes! Then I turned to the crowd and declared that our legacy would be different from the legacy my father had passed on to me. This time I'm not only committed to my marriage; now I'm equipped!"

leaving a legacy

Every couple has to make a choice to "put a stake in the ground" and start a new legacy with their family. One of the greatest gifts you can give to the next generation is faithfulness and fidelity in marriage. Consider the following:

- Hope for leaving a lasting legacy is through the gospel of Jesus Christ.
- Your marriage is a picture of the gospel to a watching world.
- Marital relationships are the central glue holding civilization together.

"You are an ancestor to someone yet to come. If you live your life knowing you are an ancestor, that will change the way you make your decisions, the way you live your life, the way you love your wife."

—Albert Mohler

"Children are the living messages we send to a time we will not see."

—Neil Postman,
The Disappearance of Childhood

five essentials in leaving a legacy that will outlive you[2]

by Dennis Rainey

1) **Fear the Lord and obey [Him].** Your legacy begins in your heart, in your relationship with God. Psalm 112:1–2 reads: "How blessed is the man who fears the LORD, / Who greatly delights in His commandments. / His descendants will be mighty on earth; / [The] generation of the upright will be blessed" [NASB].

   On our first Christmas together . . . , Barbara and I [Dennis] gave a gift to God first. These sheets of paper became title deeds to our lives—to our marriage, to our hopes of having children, to our family, to our relationships, to our rights to our lives, to whatever ministry God gave us—we gave everything to [Him].

2) **Recognize the world's needs and respond with compassion and action.** In Matthew 9:36 we read: "When He [Jesus] saw the crowds, He had compassion for them." You and your [spouse] need to leave a legacy by being committed to doing something about our world. Many Christians today are walking in the middle of the road; they're so focused on what other people think that they are unwilling to take any risks in order to make an impact for Christ. In light of this, Jamie Buckingham wrote, "The problem with Christians today is that no one wants to kill them anymore."

   When you fly over rows of houses, do you wonder how many people in those homes know Jesus? This year thirty million people will die without hearing the name of Christ. Hundreds of millions will pray to idols. Someone needs to reach these people with the Good News.

John F. Kennedy, in *Profiles in Courage*, described the need for courageous people: "Some men show courage throughout the whole of their lives. Others sail with the wind until the decisive moment when their conscience and events propel them into the center of the storm." If you want to leave a lasting legacy, you need to act with courage to reach out to those in need.

3) **Pray as a couple that God will use you to accomplish His purposes.** As recorded in 1 Chronicles 4:10, Jabez prayed, "Oh that thou wouldest bless me indeed, and enlarge my coast, and that thine hand might be with me, and that thou wouldest keep me from evil" (KJV).

   What did Jabez ask God to do? Bless him. Give him new turf and enlarge his sphere of influence. Keep him from temptation. Stay with him. Pray this prayer with your [spouse], and at the end of the year, see how different your lives will be.

4) **Help your [spouse] be a better steward of his gifts and abilities.** Help [your spouse] recognize how God has used his gifts and abilities in the past. Serving others? Teaching the Scripture[s]? Advising a Christian ministry?

   Help him plug into the local church, which needs committed laymen and women who have strong, godly character and a vision for their communities.

   Help him recognize his convictions. Thomas Carlyle says, "Conviction is worthless until it can convert itself into daily conduct." Help your mate determine what he is willing to die for so he can ultimately determine what he can live for.

5) **Ask God to give your children a sense of purpose, direction, and mission.** The challenge here is to leave your children a heritage, not just an inheritance. As someone once said, "Our children are the living messages we send to a time we will not see."

Dignity Through Destiny

David Livingstone, the missionary to Africa, said, "I will go anywhere, as long as it is forward." And by moving forward and advancing God's kingdom, he undoubtedly also advanced his sense of dignity.

Gaining a vision and a direction in life will yield significance to your [spouse's] life as well, especially if the omnipotent God of the universe has set that heading and direction. In fact, true vision, direction, and destiny can come only from the One who controls not only the present but also the future. By discovering your eternal destiny, you will begin to build lasting dignity in your lives. The internal awareness of that God-ordained dignity will enhance the self-esteem of every member of your family.

The challenge is the same for all of us. Will we follow Christ and fulfill [His] call and vision for our lives? Just as we found spiritual life in no other Person than Jesus Christ, so we find a dignity like no other in the destiny [He] provides.

Every MAN leaves a lasting INFLUENCE THAT WILL affect future generations for centuries to come.

NOT ALL LEGACIES ARE THE same. what kind of a legacy WILL YOU LEAVE BEHIND?

a spiritual LEGACY is one that MONEY can't buy AND TAXES can't take away.

A spiritual LEGACY is passing down to the next GENERATION WHAT MATTERS MOST.

Steven J. Lawson—*The Legacy*

living a life worthy of legacy[3]

A husband and wife who walked by faith and, consequently, left a legacy far beyond anything they could have imagined, lived in the early 1700s in colonial America. Their names were Jonathan and Sarah Edwards.

Jonathan Edwards felt God's call to become a minister. He and his young bride began a pastorate in a small congregation. During the years that followed, he wrote many sermons, prayers, and books, and was influential in beginning the Great Awakening. Together they produced eleven children who grew into adulthood. Sarah was a partner in her husband's ministry, and he sought her advice regarding sermons and church matters. They spent time talking about these things together, and, when their children were old enough, the parents included them in the discussions.

The effects of the Edwards's lives have been far-reaching, but the most measurable results of their faithfulness to God's call is found through their descendants. Elizabeth Dodds records a study done by A. E. Winship in 1900 in which he lists a few of the accomplishments of the 1,400 Edwards descendants he was able to find:[4]

- 100 lawyers and a dean of a law school
- 80 holders of public office
- 66 physicians and a dean of a medical school
- 65 professors of colleges and universities
- 30 judges
- 13 college presidents
- 3 mayors of large cities
- 3 governors of states
- 3 United States senators
- 1 controller of the United States Treasury
- 1 Vice President of the United States

What kind of legacy will you and your [spouse] leave? Will it be lasting? Will it be imperishable and eternal? Or will you leave behind only tangible items—buildings, money, and/or possessions?

The apostle Paul instructed Timothy to invest his life in faithful men who would be able to pass God's truth on to the next generation. Where does God want you and your mate to invest the time you have been given?

what will you leave your children?

Author and Bible teacher, Randy Alcorn, believes that Christian couples should think carefully about the kind of financial inheritance they leave to their children. He offers the following guidelines for giving an inheritance:[5]

- **Don't leave large amounts of money to your children:** It will likely do them more harm than good. "The vast majority of people who inherit wealth are living fine right now," Alcorn says. "And then this money comes to them . . . and they're not prepared to handle it. Instead of giving it away, investing it in God's kingdom . . . they're just increasing their standard of living and become dependent . . . on a higher standard of living."

- **Give it away before you die:** Instead of leaving it up to your kids, Randy says, "Why don't you give most of it away since God has entrusted it to you[,] not to them?" Experience the joy of seeing the fruit of your giving while you are still around to see it.

- **Use your money to help your children get started in a career:** Give "that which is helpful and necessary to launch them and get them started in careers." Use money to help with things such as education, training, tools, and equipment that will allow them to provide for themselves.

- **Leave a spiritual heritage:** "The most important thing that we can leave our children is not an inheritance; it's a heritage. . . . It's an example in prayer and Bible study and communication and asking forgiveness and grace and truth that have been built into the home and [provide] an example of giving."

- **Trust that God will provide for your children's needs:** "Let's not get in the way of God's work in their [lives]. . . . Let God take care of the major capital issues in their lives. . . . Help out where [you] can but not in a way that's going to interfere and . . . change their [lifestyles]."

a fitting farewell

"There were two evil brothers. They were rich, and used their money to keep their ways from the public eye. They even attended the same church, and looked to be perfect Christians. Then, their pastor retired, and a new one was hired. Not only could he see right through the brothers' deception, but he also spoke well and true. All of a sudden, one of the brothers died. The remaining brother sought out the new pastor the day before the funeral and handed him a check for the church. 'I have only one condition,' he said. 'At his funeral, you must say my brother was a saint.' The pastor gave his word, and deposited the check. The next day, at the funeral, the pastor did not hold back. 'He was an evil man,' he said. 'He cheated on his wife and abused his family.' After going on in this vein for a small time, he concluded with, 'But, compared to his brother, he was a saint.'"[6]

famous last words . . .

**"I am about to—
or I am going to—die:
either expression is correct."**

—**Dominique Bouhours,** French grammarian

"I'm so bored with it all."

—**Winston Churchill,** before slipping into a coma. He died nine days later.

"I have tried so hard to do right."

—**Grover Cleveland**

"Don't you dare ask God to help me."

—**Joan Crawford,** to her housekeeper, who had begun to pray aloud.

"I am not [in] the least afraid to die."

—**Charles Darwin**

"All my possessions for a moment of time."

—**Queen Elizabeth I of England**

"Oh, do not cry—be good children, and we shall all meet in heaven."

—**Andrew Jackson**

"Let us cross over the river and rest under the shade of the trees."

—**General Thomas "Stonewall" Jackson,** killed in error by his own troops at the battle of Chancellorsville, Virginia, during the U.S. Civil War.

"I die hard, but I am not afraid to go."

—**George Washington**

"Go away. I'm all right!"

—**H. G. Wells**

"I am ready."

—**Woodrow Wilson**

"Put out the light."

—**Theodore Roosevelt**

"Et tu, Brute?"

—**Julius Caesar,** assassinated

"Am I dying, or is this my birthday?"

—**Lady Nancy Astor,** when she woke briefly during her last illness and found all her family around her bedside.

what would you WANT said at your funeral?

take it to heart

1) What would you hope that someone from each of the following groups would say about you at your funeral? Write a sentence as if someone from each group were engraving it on your headstone:

Family

Coworkers

Neighbors or church friends

2) Identify one thing you would need to change in your life today to make all of those statements true.

a legacy OF Love

This story originally appeared in The Family Room, *which inspired the short film shown during* The Art of Marriage *event.*

"I've Never Once Stopped Loving You"[7]

Sometimes our lives are affected by unexpected and unlikely encounters. For Rich Frischkorn, one of these encounters occurred when he was a young man.

Rich patrolled a neighborhood where a couple in their late nineties lived. He regularly parked his cruiser under a massive ficus tree growing at the corner of the elderly couple's property. With its huge spread of branches, the tree provided welcome shade as he sat in his patrol car and completed his daily reports. If the elderly couple were out in their yard, they'd walk over to him and talk.

As time passed, he noticed there was something very different about the aging husband and wife—the way they looked at one another and smiled . . . the way they worked in their yard together . . . the way their hands interlocked on their evening strolls.

One day the young deputy sheriff observed the elderly man mowing a neighbor's yard. Almost one hundred years of age, he later told Rich that he was helping because the woman was "too old" to mow her own grass.

Rich watched the couple pick up mail for neighbors who were out of town. He saw them drive friends to a store or doctor's office. He anticipated their offers of cold lemonade or tea on hot afternoons.

In Christ's Name

He wondered about the source of the couple's love and care. Over time he learned the answer: all was done in Christ's name.

Their curiosity about Rich's spiritual condition touched him. They'd often comment that he was in a dangerous job and would ask, "Do you know where you will spend eternity?"

He'd answer that he'd probably end up in hell. And they would say that he could avoid that.

One day when Rich was filling out reports, the elderly woman tapped on the window of his cruiser. She held a vase with freshly picked flowers.

She told him to look at the flowers—really look. Then she asked if he thought the flowers could have been created by chance. "No," she told the young officer. "God made these for us to look at, marvel at, and wonder."

All Rich could do was gaze at the woman with the lined face and say that she was right.

Day after day Rich patrolled the neighborhood. He watched the aging couple pull weeds together in their flowerbeds, never more than an arm's length apart. One would reach out and touch the other. They'd look at each other, smile, and nod, and then go back to pulling weeds. Rich thought, *How much in love.*

Rich and the couple became more than friends. They treated him as part of their family. He joined two hundred to three hundred people at their eighty-first, eighty-second, and eighty-third anniversary celebrations.

He laughed to himself when he realized that their children were in their sixties and seventies, and some of their grandchildren were in their early fifties.

The Phone Call He Didn't Want to Receive

As the years went by, Rich feared that the couple's time on earth was short. He dreaded the day when one of them would pass away. At that time in Florida, if someone died at home, a deputy had to come and do a report.

Sure enough, one evening Rich received a phone call saying there had been a death at the elderly couple's house. Wanting to be anywhere but their home, he pulled into the driveway.

He knocked on the door of their two-story house with cedar siding.

"Who is it?" the wife asked.

"It's the sheriff's department."

"Rich, is that you?"

"Yes, it is," he answered.

"Oh, praise the Lord; I've been praying a friend would come."

Rich stepped into the house and saw the elderly couple sitting side by side on the couch. She wore a faded, swirled-patterned dress, and her husband had on work pants and a checkered, short-sleeved shirt. His hands were folded in his lap, his chin was on his chest, and he had a pleasant look on his face—as though he were in the middle of a good dream.

"Can you tell me what happened?" Rich asked.

She said her husband had been sick the past couple of weeks. That evening they were watching the news, and he started having a little trouble breathing. She asked if he wanted her to phone the doctor, and he replied, "No, everything is going to be fine."

But it wasn't fine—his breathing got worse. She rose to call an ambulance, and he grabbed her hand with unusual strength.

"You may not believe me, Rich," she continued, "but he was a young man again. And his face was just glowing, and he was smiling, and he said, 'Don't go—sit here next to me.'"

So she sat back down and heard these final words from her husband: "In all these years together, I've never once stopped loving you. And I love you more today than all of the days gone by. But my Father is calling now, and I have to go home. But we'll be together again soon, and until then know that I'm waiting for you and know that I love you. Good-bye."

With that, his head dropped onto his chest, and he was gone.

"He's in heaven with our Lord and Savior, and I will be too," she told Rich. "And one day you can be there."

The ambulance crew arrived shortly after their conversation. Rich remembers her telling them, "He's home with the Lord. He's home with Jesus."

Living Color

Although more than thirty years have passed since Rich's life intersected with the elderly couple, their example was stamped in living color on his heart. Rich eventually gave his life over to the Lord and became a Christian. "They planted the seeds [of faith] in my heart," he says.

Whenever he talks about the elderly couple, he mentions their rock-solid faith and how they lived it day after day. "They were always witnessing and reaching out to others," he says, "and yet they were never preachy, never pushy. It was just something I wanted to emulate."

The last time Rich saw the old woman, she was more than one hundred years old. She was on her hands and knees pulling weeds in her flowerbeds.

"Every once in a while," Rich says, "she'd reach out with her arm, smile, and nod, and then go back to pulling weeds."

COMPLETING *the Picture*

- I must think about the impact of my life on future generations.
- My hope for leaving a lasting legacy is through the gospel of Jesus Christ.
- I will begin to leave a godly legacy by "putting a stake in the ground" today.

take it to heart

leaving a legacy for generations to come

Every person leaves a legacy. The question is, What kind of legacy will it be? You have an opportunity right now to begin recording the kind of legacy you hope to leave for future generations.

Your charge is to write a letter that expresses your convictions on the importance of marriage and family. Imagine one of the following situations in which a letter from you might be read:

- a wedding for one of your grandchildren, great-grandchildren, or even great-great-grandchildren that you aren't able to attend
- the day when your closest family and friends have gathered to honor you—the day of your funeral
- a time one hundred years from now, long after you're gone, when some family member just happens to be looking through your belongings and stumbles across this letter

Select one of these three scenarios and ask yourself a few questions:

- What would you want in that letter?
- What are the most important things you would want to leave behind for future generations to read?
- What are some of your life experiences that have shaped your convictions about the importance of marriage and family?
- What passages of Scripture has God used in your life that you would want to highlight?

In your letter, you may want to include some of the following:

1) Mention that you were attending a marriage event when you were prompted to write the letter. Write about some of the things you learned this weekend that you would want your loved ones to know, such as

   a. any key principles or scriptures that were shared,

   b. some of the more important teachings, and

   c. a memorable quote or saying you heard.

   Feel free to look back through your book to locate a few of these things.

2) Every legacy, no matter how apparently glorious, has spots of tarnish; there are always regrets, mistakes, and things that could have been done differently. No one can change the past, but you can begin to change the future and the legacy you leave from this point forward. In your letter, you may want to acknowledge mistakes you have made. Talk about what you would have done differently if given the chance.

3) Capture any additional thoughts you would want to leave a future generation, such as

   a. memorable moments in your life or stories about your experiences,

   b. examples from people you admired (grandparents, mentors, etc.),

   c. good books you recommend, or

   d. "life verses" or important Scripture verses.

4) Close the letter with a blessing or an encouragement to your loved ones to pursue a godly legacy.

leaving a legacy for generations to come

Make sure to write your letter focusing on one of the three specific situations described earlier. Once you're finished, seal the letter in an envelope, and make sure that others in your extended family know about this letter so that it can be read someday on the occasion you chose. Put it somewhere for safekeeping (such as a fireproof safe or a bank-deposit box).

To help you get started on your letter, we've provided the following example of how it might begin. (Feel free to use the opening paragraph as a template for your letter.)

Your mom [or Dad] and I just spent the past twenty-four hours attending an event called The Art of Marriage, where we've learned more about what the Bible teaches concerning marriage. While we've been here, I've been reminded of how important it is in life to pass on a legacy of spiritual vitality to those who are still alive after I'm gone. So I'm writing this letter to share with you some of the things I've learned in my life that will help you live in a way that honors God in your marriage and family.

One of the things I learned this weekend was . . .

Of course, I haven't been perfect, and I don't have it all figured out. I need to ask your forgiveness for . . .

But know that my prayer for you is . . .

a legacy pledge

Recognizing that our relationship with each other is a critical part of the spiritual legacy God has called us to pass on to the next generation, and that God has placed within us a desire for purpose, meaning, and significance, we make this pledge today, before God, to move forward in building a lasting legacy for our family and the generations to follow:

Husband's Pledge

I pledge to you today that, with God's help, I will make our marriage the priority it is meant to be. I will love and lead you. I will protect and provide for you. I will nourish and cherish you.

Wife's Pledge

I pledge to you today that, with God's help, I will make our marriage the priority it is meant to be. I will be your helper and encourager. I will respect you. I will support you and cheer you on.

Husband and Wife Pledge

We will remember that our commitment to each other will have an impact on future generations. We will persevere through painful times and press on to the end of our lives together. We will live for something greater than our own brief existence. From this day forward, our marriage will be more about leaving a lasting legacy than pacifying our passing pleasures.

We commit, from this day forward, to put a "stake in the ground." We give our lives completely over to God—every dream, every possession, every relationship—and ask Him to guide us in every decision we make, for His sake and for the sake of our family and the generations that will be affected by the choices we make this day.

SIGN: ______________________________ DATE: ______________

SIGN: ______________________________ DATE: ______________

WITNESS: ______________________________

WITNESS: ______________________________

notes

SESSION 1

1. Bill Adler, ed., "When I Get Married," *McCall's*, June 1979, 107, quoted in Dennis Rainey and Barbara Rainey, *Staying Close* (Nashville: Thomas Nelson, 2003), 109.

2. Relationships Australia and Credit Union Australia, *Relationships Indicators Survey 2008: Issues and Concerns That Australians Have in Their Relationships Today* (Deakin, ACT, Australia: Relationships Australia, 2008), 13, relationships.com.au/resources/pdfs/reports-submissions/ra-rel-ind-survey-2008-report.pdf.

3. Paula Y. Goodwin, William D. Mosher, and Anjani Chandra, "Marriage and Cohabitation in the United States: A Statistical Portrait Based on Cycle 6 (2002) of the National Survey of Family Growth," National Center for Health Statistics, *Vital Health Statistics* 23, no. 28 (2010): 2, www.cdc.gov/nchs/data/series/sr_23/sr23_028.pdf.

4. Ibid., 19, 35, 36.

5. Adapted from Dave Boehi, "Five Things I Wish I'd Known Before Marriage," Marriage Memo, FamilyLife.com, October 19, 2009, www.familylife.com/site/apps/nlnet/content3.aspx?c=dnJHKLNnFoG&b=3871747&ct=7515727.

6. Summarized from *The Complete Works of Francis A. Schaeffer: A Christian Worldview* (Wheaton, IL: Crossway, 1982), 1:78–79.

7. "Wedding Budget vs. Real Wedding Cost," Cost of Wedding, accessed October 12, 2010, costofwedding.com.

8. Scott Williams, independent survey of ten premarital counseling centers across the United States, April 2010.

9. Scott M. Stanley, Paul R. Amato, Christine A. Johnson, and Howard J. Markman, "Premarital Education, Marital Quality, and Marital Stability: Findings from a Large, Random Household Survey," *Journal of Family Psychology* 20, no. 1 (2006): 117–26.

10. Dennis Rainey and Barbara Rainey, *Starting Your Marriage Right* (Nashville: Thomas Nelson, 2000), 15–18. Reprinted by permission.

SESSION 2

1. John Gottman, *Why Marriages Succeed or Fail: And How You Can Make Yours Last* (New York: Simon and Schuster, 1995), 29.

2. Adapted from Dennis Rainey and Barbara Rainey, *Starting Your Marriage Right* (Nashville: Thomas Nelson, 2000), 43–46. Used by permission.

SESSION 3

1. Tim Satchell, *Astaire: The Biography* (London: Arrow, 1988), 127.

2. John Mueller, "She Changed Partners and Danced," *New York Times,* October 20, 1991, nytimes.com/ 1991/10/20/books/she-changed-partners-and-danced.html.

3. Winnie Ooi, "Taking the Lead in Ballroom Latin Dance: The Role of a Leader in a Dance Partnership," Suite101®.com, June 30, 2009, www.suite101.com/content/taking-the-lead-in-ballroom-latin-dance-a128503. Used by permission.

4. Taken from *Cosmopolitan* magazine, "Describe Your Perfect Man," Cosmo Chat, cosmopolitan.co.uk/chatroom/topic/43628.

5. Giles Coren et al., "What Makes an Ideal Woman?" *Sunday Times,* September 28, 2008, www.timesonline.co.uk/tol/life_and_style/men/article4790198.ece.

6. Adapted from Dennis Rainey and Barbara Rainey, *Starting Your Marriage Right* (Nashville: Thomas Nelson, 2000), 7–9. Used by permission.

7. Yahoo! HotJobs annual job-satisfaction survey, cited in "Top 10 Qualities of a Good Boss," RISMedia, January 10, 2008, www.rismedia.com/2008-01-09/top-10-qualities-of-a-good-boss/.

8. Adapted from Dennis Rainey and Barbara Rainey, *Building Your Mate's Self-Esteem* (Nashville: Thomas Nelson, 1995), 250. Used by permission.

9. Wayne Grudem, *Evangelical Feminism and Biblical Truth* (Sisters, OR: Multnomah, 2004), 544.

10. Wayne and Margaret Grudem, interview by Bob Lepine, March 10, 2010.

11. Adapted from Dennis Rainey, "25 Ways to Spiritually Lead Your Family," FamilyLife, accessed November 11, 2010, www.familylife.com/site/apps/nlnet/content3.aspx?c=dnJHKLNnFoG&b=3871753&ct=4640205.

12. Summarized and quoted from a speech by C. J. Mahaney, "What to Do When a Wife Won't Submit," Building Strong Families in Your Church Pastors Conference (Dallas: March 2000).

13. Adapted from Dennis Rainey and Barbara Rainey, "A Wife's Job Description," FamilyLife, accessed October 21, 2010,www.familylife.com/site/apps/nlnet/content3.aspx?c=dnJHKLNnFoG&b=3781105&ct=4639815.

14. Summarized and quoted from a speech by Bunny Wilson, "Liberating Submission," Building Strong Families in Your Church Pastors Conference (Dallas: March 2000).

15. Adapted from Rainey, *Building Your Mate's Self-Esteem*, 181.

16. Kathy Thibodeaux, interview by Scott Williams, May 2010.

17. Dennis Rainey and Barbara Rainey, "Q&A: Making Decisions When You Disagree," FamilyLife, accessed October 21, 2010, www.familylife.com/site/apps/nlnet/content3.aspx?c=dnJHKLNnFoG&b=3781085&ct=4639753.

SESSION 4

1. *Merriam-Webster's Collegiate Dictionary*, 11th ed., s.v. "hedonism."

2. List taken from William DeJong, U.S. Department of Justice, National Institute of Justice, *Building the Peace: The Resolving Conflict Creatively Program* (Washington, DC: Government Printing Office, 1993), NCJ-149549, 6.

3. Dennis Rainey and Barbara Rainey, "Q&A: Should Children See Parents Argue?" FamilyLife, accessed November 11, 2010, www.familylife.com/site/apps/nlnet/content3.aspx?c=dnJHKLNnFoG&b=3855925&ct=4639787.

4. Adapted from Jon Meacham, *Franklin and Winston: An Intimate Portrait of an Epic Friendship* (New York: Random House, 2003), 64–65.

5. Crawford W. Loritts Jr., *Lessons from a Life Coach: You Are Created to Make a Difference* (Chicago: Moody, 2001), 76–77. Used by permission.

SESSION 5

1. David P. Barash, "Deflating the Myth of Monogamy," posted on Trinity University's 2004 "Identity and Integrity" course syllabus, Department of Religion, accessed October 26, 2010, www.trinity.edu/rnadeau/fys/barash%20on%20monogamy.htm.

2. Adapted from C. J. Mahaney, *Sex, Romance, and the Glory of God* (Wheaton, IL: Crossway, 2004), 11–13.

3. Adapted from Dennis Rainey and Barbara Rainey, "Q&A: When Your Child Invades Your Relationship," FamilyLife, accessed October 26, 2010, www.familylife.com/site/apps/nlnet/content3.aspx?c=dnJHKLNnFoG&b=3781093&ct=4639581.

4. From The Barna Group, "Morality Continues to Decay," November 3, 2003, www.barna.org/barna-update/article/5-barna-update/129-morality-continues-to-decay.

5. Survey conducted by ChristiaNet, Inc., cited in "ChristiaNet Poll Finds that Evangelicals Are Addicted to Porn," *Market Wire*, August 7, 2006, www.marketwire.com/press-release/ChristiaNet-Poll-Finds-That-Evangelicals-Are-Addicted-to-Porn-703951.htm.

6. Mark A. Yarhouse, "Marriage Related Research," *Christian Counseling Today* 12, no. 1 (2004), cited in Covenant Eyes, "Pornography Statistics," accessed September 10, 2010, www.covenanteyes.com/help_and_support/pdfs/Covenant%20Eyes%20Pornography%20Statistics.pdf.

7. From Jennifer P. Schneider, "Effects of Cybersex Addiction on the Family: Results of a Survey," *Sexual Addiction and Compulsivity* 7 (2000): 31–58, www.jenniferschneider.com/articles/cybersex_family.html.

8. Najah S. Musacchio, Molly Hartrich, and Robert Garofalo, "Erectile Dysfunction and Viagra Use: What's Up with College-Age Males?" *Journal of Adolescent Health* 39 (2006): 452–54, cited in Leonard Sax, *Boys Adrift* (New York: Basic Books, 2007), 132.

9. Dave Boehi, "Breaking Free from the Trap of Pornography," accessed October 26, 2010, www.familylife.com/site/apps/nlnet/content3.aspx?c=dnJHKLNnFoG&b=3576485&ct=4637893&notoc=1.

10. Adapted from Boehi, "Breaking Free from the Trap of Pornography."

11. Ann Botash, "Examination for Sexual Abuse in Prepubertal Children: An Update," *Pediatric Annual* (May 1997), cited in the National Center for Victims of Crime, "Child Sexual Abuse," www.ncvc.org/ncvc/main.aspx?dbName=DocumentViewer&DocumentID=32315.

12. Howard N. Snyder, *Sexual Assault of Young Children as Reported to Law Enforcement* (Washington, D.C.: Government Printing Office, Bureau of Justice Statistics, 2000), 10, http://bjs.ojp.usdoj.gov/content/pub/pdf/saycrle.pdf.

13. World Health Organization, *World Report on Violence and Health* (Geneva: World Health Organization, 2002), accessed November 16, 2010, whqlibdoc.who.int/publications/2002/9241545615_chap6_eng.pdf.

14. "The Rise of Viagra, and Overcoming Male Sexual Performance Anxiety Without It," *Sex Health Review* (January 22, 2010), accessed September 10, 2010, http://sex-health-review.com/the-rise-of-viagra-and-overcoming-male-sexual-performance-anxiety-without-it.

15. William Cutrer and Sandra Glahn, *Sexual Intimacy in Marriage* (Grand Rapids: Kregel, 2007), 111–112.

16. Archibald Hart, Ph.D., Catherine Hart Weber, Ph.D., and Debra Taylor, M.A., *Secrets of Eve: Understanding the Mystery of Female Sexuality* (Nashville: Word, 1998), 43.

17. Adapted from Dennis Rainey and Barbara Rainey, *Rekindling the Romance* (Nashville: Thomas Nelson, 2004), 255–61. Used by permission.

18. Ibid., 57–67.

19. Adapted from Dennis Rainey and Barbara Rainey, *Building Your Mate's Self Esteem* (Nashville: Thomas Nelson, 1995), 253–70. Used by permission.

20. Jill Renich, *To Have and to Hold* (Grand Rapids: Zondervan, 1975), 55.

SESSION 6

1. Mary May Larmoyeux, "10 Ideas: Helping Your Marriage Last a Lifetime," FamilyLife, accessed October 28, 2010, www.familylife.com/site/apps/nlnet/content3.aspx?c=dnJHKLNnFoG&b=3781065&ct=5722439.

2. Adapted from Dennis Rainey and Barbara Rainey, *Building Your Mate's Self-Esteem* (Nashville: Thomas Nelson, 1995), 230–232. Reprinted by permission.

3. Rainey, *Building Your Mate's Self-Esteem*, 229.

4. Study conducted in 1900 by A. E. Winship, cited in Elizabeth Dodds, "Marriage to a Difficult Man" in *Where Have all the Mothers Gone?* Brenda Hunter (Grand Rapids, MI: Zondervan, 1982), 109.

5. Summarized and quoted from Randy Alcorn, interview by Dennis Rainey and Bob Lepine, "We're in the Money–Now What? There's More to Money Than Spending," *FamilyLife Today*, November 21, 2005.

6. K. S. Bhalla, *Let's Laugh, Mister Smile* (Delhi, India: Global Vision, 2005), 150.

7. Adapted from Mary May Larmoyeux, "I've Never Once Stopped Loving You," FamilyLife, accessed October 27, 2010, www.familylife.com/site/apps/nlnet/content3.aspx?c=dnJHKLNnFoG&b=3584679&ct=6356261.

the art of marriage team

Pam Abell

Pam and her husband, Barry, serve as the directors of Executive Ministries New Jersey, an affiliated ministry of Campus Crusade for Christ. Together they lead Bible studies, retreats, and mentoring weekends for engaged and married couples. Pam received a Master's of Science degree in elementary education.

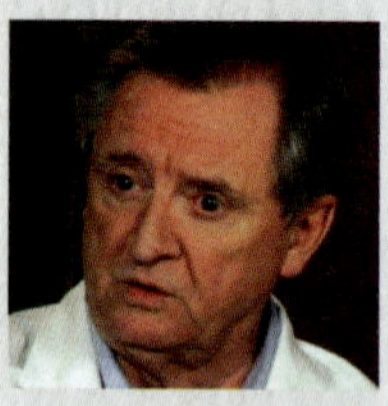

Jim Arkins

James Arkins, M.D., is a family physician who lives in Bella Vista, Arkansas. His medical practice included marriage counseling and treatment of sexual dysfunction. Recently retired, Jim now devotes his time to caring for the needy, homeless, and uninsured, serving as a medical missionary and encouraging others in their walk with Christ. He and his wife, Anne, have been married forty-five years. They are the parents of four and the grandparents of eleven.

Jose and Michelle Alvarez

Jose played professional baseball for sixteen years and began competing professionally in golf in 2006. He is part of the Fellowship of Christian Athletes Golf Ministry serving in several capacities, including chaplain for the Nationwide Tour and assisting in national outreach events. Michelle works with an event planning and management team and is an administrative assistant.

Voddie Baucham

Dr. Voddie Baucham Jr. wears many hats. He is a husband, father, pastor, author, professor, conference speaker, and church planter. He currently serves as pastor of preaching at Grace Family Baptist Church in Spring, Texas. He and his wife, Bridget, have six children.

Bruce and Julie Boyd

Bruce and Julie serve in the concert and arts outreach of Campus Crusade for Christ's Keynote ministry. The Boyds, with their children, minister through music at events that focus on family and marriage issues. Bruce received his Bachelor of Arts degree in music education from the University of Illinois. Julie received a Bachelor's degree in Business Management from Texas Wesleyan University, and now home schools their three boys.

Bryan Carter

Bryan L. Carter (M.A., Dallas Theological Seminary) is the senior pastor of Concord Church in Dallas, Texas. He is active in the city of Dallas in numerous capacities and hosts a national conference on expository preaching. He is married to his college sweetheart, Stephanie; they have three children.

Raymond and Donna Causey

Raymond, former director of Urban Family Ministries, now pastors a church in Atlanta. He received his Bachelor of Arts in communications and biblical studies from Biola University, and authored *Changing for Good*. His wife, Donna, is a homemaker, Bible teacher, and mentor.

Bobby Conway

Bobby, his wife, Heather, and their two children live in Huntersville, North Carolina, where they moved to start a church in 2004. Today Bobby serves as the lead pastor of Life Fellowship. He received his master's degree from Dallas Theological Seminary and his doctorate from Southern Evangelical Seminary.

Chuck and Melissa Douglas

Chuck and Melissa have served with FamilyLife since 2001. Prior to that, Chuck spent over eleven years on the Oklahoma City Police Department. Chuck and Melissa oversee the field ministry of FamilyLife in the southeast and also serve pastors and church leaders as they develop family ministry within their congregations. They have four children.

Michael Easley

Dr. Michael Easley is an author, speaker, former president of the Moody Bible Institute, pastor, and conference speaker. Michael and his wife, Cindy, have four children and live near Nashville, Tennessee, where Michael serves as the lead pastor of Fellowship Bible Church.

Brian and Jen Goins

Brian and Jennifer Goins work with couples in Charlotte, North Carolina, where Brian is a pastor at Renaissance Bible Church. He also writes for various non-profit organizations. Jennifer is a homemaker who enjoys leading Bible study groups, cooking, and keeping track of her family's memories and milestones. The Goinses have three children.

Wayne and Margaret Grudem

Wayne Grudem is a research professor of theology and biblical studies at Phoenix Seminary. He was a member of the translation oversight committee for the English Standard Version of the Bible and general editor for the ESV Study Bible. Margaret is a full-time homemaker and leads discipleship groups for wives of pastors. The Grudems have three grown sons and two grandchildren.

Dave Harvey

Dr. Dave Harvey (D. Min., Westminster Theological Seminary) is responsible for church planting, church care, and international expansion for Sovereign Grace Ministries, having served on the leadership team since 1995. He is the author of *When Sinners Say "I Do"* and is a contributing author to *Worldliness: Resisting the Seduction of a Fallen World*. Dave lives in West Chester, Pennsylvania, with his wife, Kimm. They have four children.

Mary Kassian

Mary Kassian is an award-winning author, internationally renowned speaker, and a distinguished professor at The Southern Baptist Theological Seminary. She has published several books and Bible studies, including *The Feminist Mistake*. A graduate of Rehabilitation Medicine from the University of Alberta, Canada, Mary has also studied systematic theology at the doctoral level and taught courses at seminaries throughout North America.

Bryan Loritts

Bryan is the lead pastor of Fellowship Memphis Church, a multicultural church ministering to the urban Memphis community. Bryan has a master's degree in theology and is currently working on his Ph.D. In addition to serving the community of Memphis, Bryan's ministry takes him across the country as a speaker. He wrote *God on Paper* and was a contributing author to *Great Preaching*. Bryan and his wife, Korie, have three sons.

Crawford Loritts

Dr. Crawford Loritts is the senior pastor of Fellowship Bible Church in Roswell, Georgia, the daily host of the radio program "Living a Legacy," internationally known Bible teacher, and author. His books include *A Passionate Commitment, Leadership as an Identity,* and *Never Walk Away*. Crawford and his bride, Karen, have been married forty years. They have four grown children and five grandchildren.

Robyn McKelvy

Robyn and her husband, Ray, live in Brentwood, Tennessee, where Ray serves as a community group pastor at Fellowship Bible Church. Robyn, a mother of eight children, keeps busy with cooking, cleaning, laundry, counseling, mentoring, and writing. She has finished her first book and awaits its publication.

Tony and Venita Mitchell

Tony is chief financial officer of Morrison Management Specialists. He is a Certified Public Accountant (CPA), a board member of a national food service non-profit organization, and a public speaker. Venita, also a CPA, has worked in public and private accounting, is director of women's ministry at her local church, and has been a full-time homemaker since 1988.

Al Mohler

Dr. R. Albert Mohler Jr. serves as president of the Southern Baptist Theological Seminary. A leader among American evangelicals, Dr. Mohler is widely sought as a columnist and cultural commentator. He is the author of numerous books, including *Words from the Fire*, and is the host of two programs, *Thinking in Public* and *The Briefing*. He also writes a popular blog. He is married to Mary; they have two children.

Hans and Star Molegraaf

Hans and Star have a powerful testimony of God's ability to revive a dead marriage. They served with FamilyLife for four years and now provide marriage help to hurting couples through their own marriage ministry, Marriage Revolution. They and their six children live near Houston, Texas.

Russell Moore

Russell D. Moore is the senior vice president for Academic Administration and dean of the school of theology at The Southern Baptist Theological Seminary in Louisville, Kentucky. He is also a preaching pastor at Highview Baptist Church in Louisville, a writer *(Adopted for Life)* and speaker. He is a senior editor of *Touchstone: A Journal of Mere Christianity* and also blogs regularly at russellmoore.com. He and his wife, Maria, have four sons.

Tim Muehlhoff

Dr. Tim Muehlhoff (Ph.D., University of North Carolina at Chapel Hill) has been on staff with Campus Crusade for Christ since 1986 and currently teaches classes in interpersonal communication, rhetoric, and family communication at Biola University. He is the author of *Marriage Forecasting, Authentic Communication,* and *The God Conversation* (with J. P. Moreland). Tim and his wife, Noreen, are frequent speakers at FamilyLife marriage conferences. They live in Brea, California, with their three sons.

Bill and Pam Mutz

Bill is the president of Lakeland Automall in Lakeland, Florida. He has been involved with the ministries of FamilyLife and Promise Keepers. Bill and Pam serve in their local church and various community boards. Pam graduated as a physical education major and is a commissioned Centurion through Prison Fellowship. She currently mentors and teaches women's Bible studies. Bill and Pam are the parents of twelve children.

Dennis and Barbara Rainey

Dr. Dennis Rainey serves as president of FamilyLife® and hosts the nationally syndicated *FamilyLife® Today* radio program. Barbara is an artist and writer, and enjoys creating resources for women and families. The Raineys have written over twenty-five books together, including bestsellers *Moments Together for Couples* and *Building Your Mate's Self-Esteem*. They have six children and numerous grandchildren.

Jeff and Debbie Schreve

Jeff is the senior pastor of First Baptist Church in Texarkana, Texas, and the founder of the radio and TV ministry, From His Heart Ministries. Debbie is a housewife and works as the executive secretary for From His Heart Ministries.

Jeff Schulte

Jeff is a Fellow and Executive Director of the Sage Hill Institute, an initiative for authentic Christian leadership. He speaks nationally and internationally on a variety of men's issues including biblical masculinity, fatherhood, spiritual formation, leadership, and relational authenticity. Jeff and his wife, Brenda, are the parents of six children and reside in Anchorage, Alaska.

Bobby Scott

Bobby Scott is the teaching pastor of Los Angeles Community Bible Church, instructor at the Los Angeles Bible Training School, and a visiting lecturer at The Master's Seminary. He holds a M.Div. and Th.M. from The Master's Seminary. Scott is the general editor of *Secret Sex Wars*, a biblical anthology from seven Christian leaders. He cherishes his family—his devoted wife, Naomi, and their six children.

Paul David Tripp

Dr. Paul Tripp has been a church planter, traveling musician, painter, teacher, author, and founder of a Christian school. He currently serves as the president of Paul Tripp Ministries, and is on the pastoral staff at Tenth Presbyterian Church in Philadelphia. He is also professor of pastoral life and care at the Redeemer Seminary in Dallas. Paul and Luella, his wife of almost forty years, have four children.

Christopher and Susan Willard

Chris and Susan Willard met at the University of Massachusetts where Chris studied history and Susan studied painting and design. Chris has an MBA and works as a consultant and coach with Leadership Network, which is dedicated to accelerating the impact of high capacity leaders. Susan is an interior decorator and owns her own business, Fabulous Interiors. They have three children and live in Orlando.

Dave and Ann Wilson

Dave received a Master of Divinity degree from the International School of Theology and serves as teaching pastor to the Kensington Community Church in Troy, Michigan. Inducted into the Men's Athletic Hall of Fame at Ball State University, Dave is also chaplain to the Detroit Lions. Ann ministers to wives of professional athletes and is a homemaker.

We enjoyed The Art of Marriage ...

what can we do next?

FamilyLife is here to help with practical, biblical resources for your marriage and family.

For your marriage

- Weekend to Remember® marriage getaway—spend a weekend with your spouse in a hotel setting and go to a deeper level in your marriage
- Marriage Oneness video series—learn how to grow in true intimacy, connection and purpose, and to experience closeness for a lifetime in this 8-week series
- HomeBuilders Couples Series®—start or join a small group with one of our HomeBuilders studies

For her

- The Life Ready Woman video series—join Shaunti Feldhahn as she shows you how to have balance, peace and joy by discovering God's blueprint for your life
- MomLifeToday.com—enjoy community with real moms experiencing every age and every stage of MomLife—right alongside you

For him

- Stepping Up: A Call to Courageous Manhood video series

For your family

- **The Smart Stepfamily video series**—family expert Ron Deal helps couples facilitate the "blending process," gives tips for raising stepkids and offers solutions for everyday living
- **FamilyLife Today® radio broadcast**—find daily encouragement on your local Christian stations
- **FamilyLife.com**—sign up to receive our free e-zine and daily devotionals

Visit FamilyLife.com for more information.

Do you need a little review?

We know we've cast quite a cluster of content at you this weekend – almost 5 ½ hours of video! If you missed any of the torrent of tips, or would just like to review the flurry of facts, you can access all the sessions from The Art of Marriage on FamilyLife's website.

Go to TheArtofMarriage.com/AfterTheEvent, fill out a brief survey, and enter the code GEN224 to access all the sessions online.

Introducing

the art of marriage®

small-group series

Adapted from the highly successful The Art of Marriage video event, The Art of Marriage Small-Group Series weaves together expert teaching, stories of real marriages and man-on-the-street interviews. This six-week series portrays the hope and beauty of God's design for marriage in a format **perfect for Sunday school groups, home Bible study groups or any other small-group setting.**

The Art of Marriage Small-Group Leader Kit includes:

- one DVD featuring six 20–25 minute video sessions
- a leader's guide
- two participant guides that include small-group discussion questions, date-night suggestions for couples, articles and more.

Order today at ShopFamilyLife.com.

ABOUT FAMILYLIFE®

FamilyLife® is a donor-supported nonprofit organization headquartered in Little Rock, Arkansas, whose mission is to develop godly marriages and families who change the world one home at a time. Cofounded in 1976 by Dennis and Barbara Rainey, FamilyLife has strengthened millions of marriages and families through numerous resources, including:

- Weekend to Remember® marriage getaway
- *FamilyLife Today*® and *Real FamilyLife® with Dennis Rainey* radio broadcasts
- HomeBuilders small-group studies
- The Art of Marriage®—a video-based marriage event
- Stepping Up™
- Passport2Purity®
- FamilyLife.com
- Hope for Orphans®

FamilyLife works in more than one hundred countries around the world and utilizes a volunteer network of more than ten thousand couples nationwide. They help bring God's message to others through the practical application of time-tested techniques and teachings that are based on biblical principles.

Through the guidance of FamilyLife's experts and with the help of their lay ministry, FamilyLife has developed into a vibrant, visionary organization that is today changing the world one home at a time.

Visit FamilyLife.com for more information.

evaluation form

Event Location: ______________________ **Event Date:** ____________

Event (Content and Facility):

The Overall Experience	Poor	1	2	3	4	5	6	7	8	9	10	Excellent
Content Quality (Sessions)	Poor	1	2	3	4	5	6	7	8	9	10	Excellent
The Schedule	Poor	1	2	3	4	5	6	7	8	9	10	Excellent
Video Quality	Poor	1	2	3	4	5	6	7	8	9	10	Excellent
Sound Quality	Poor	1	2	3	4	5	6	7	8	9	10	Excellent
Location/Venue	Poor	1	2	3	4	5	6	7	8	9	10	Excellent
Live Host	Poor	1	2	3	4	5	6	7	8	9	10	Excellent
The Manual	Poor	1	2	3	4	5	6	7	8	9	10	Excellent
Price Charged	Poor	1	2	3	4	5	6	7	8	9	10	Excellent

Please comment about the viewing experience including the venue, the video (audio and visual), host interaction, seating and lighting, etc.

Describe the effect this event has had on you and your spouse (or fiancé/fiancée).

May we quote you? ❑ yes ❑ no

Rate the health of your marriage before and after the event.

before: Poor 1 2 3 4 5 6 7 8 9 10 Excellent
after: Poor 1 2 3 4 5 6 7 8 9 10 Excellent

Would you invite someone to attend The Art of Marriage® if another event were hosted near you?
❑ yes ❑ no Why or why not?

Would you consider hosting The Art of Marriage? ❑ yes ❑ no
Why or why not?

Did you accept Jesus Christ as your savior this weekend? ❑ yes ❑ no

Did you pray to be filled with the Holy Spirit this weekend? ❑ yes ❑ no

Would you like for anyone to contact you and follow up with you about any of the spiritually significant decisions you made this weekend? ❑ yes ❑ no

Additional Comments:

Name: First ______________________ Last ______________________

Gender: ❑ Male ❑ Female Age: ❑ 20s ❑ 30s ❑ 40s ❑ 50s or older

Do you have child(ren)? ❑ yes ❑ no If so how many? ____

Ages? ❑ 0-5 ❑ 6-10 ❑ 11-13 ❑ 14-18 ❑ 19+

Phone Number: ______________ circle one: home/work/cell

E-mail(s) ______________________________________